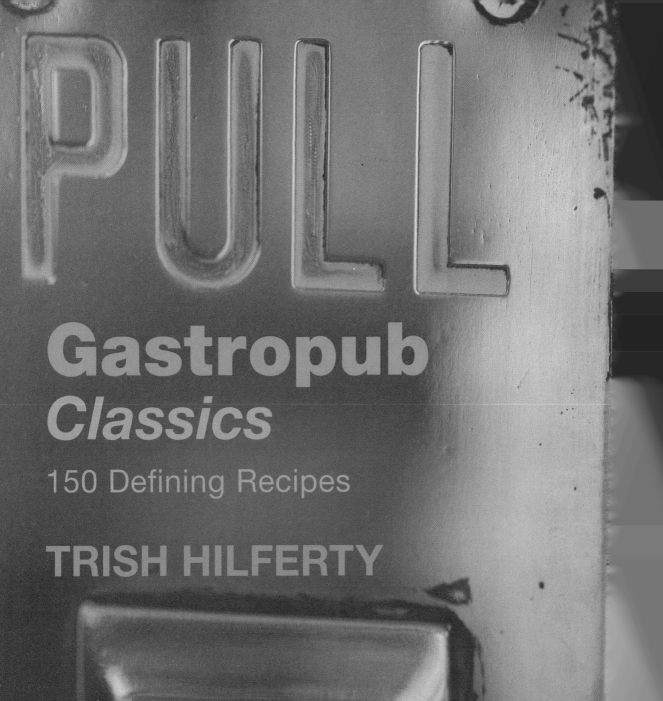

Gastropub
Classics

150 Defining Recipes

TRISH HILFERTY

For my mum, my dad and David

Gastropub
Classics

150 Defining Recipes

TRISH HILFERTY

Absolute Press

First published in Great Britain in 2006 by

Absolute Press
Scarborough House
29 James Street West
Bath BA 1 2BT
Phone 44 (0) 1225 316013
Fax 44 (0) 1225 445836
E-mail info@absolutepress.co.uk
Website www.absolutepress.co.uk

Publisher Jon Croft
Commissioning Editor Meg Avent
Designer Matt Inwood
Publishing Assistant Meg Devenish
Photographer Jason Lowe
Food Stylist Trish Hilferty

A catalogue record of this book is available
from the British Library.

ISBN: 1904573533
ISBN 13: 9781904573531

A note about the text
This book is set in Sabon, which was
designed by Jan Tschichold in 1964. The
roman design is based on type by Claude
Garamond, whereas the italic design is
based on types by Robert Granjon.

Contents

Notes for American Readers

British and American cookbooks use different measuring systems. In the UK, dry ingredients are measured by weight, with the metric system increasingly replacing the Imperial one, while in the US they are measured by volume. Below are metric equivalents for cup measurements of some common ingredients:

1 cup butter 240g	1 cup nuts 115g
1 tablespoon butter 15g	1 cup grated Cheddar-type cheese 115g
1 cup flour 150g	1 cup grated Parmesan cheese 100g
1 cup caster sugar 200g	1 cup dried beans 200g
1 cup icing sugar 140g	1 cup lentils 225g
1 cup fresh breadcrumbs 50g	1 cup rice 200g

CONVERSION TABLES

These are conversions from metric weights and measures to Imperial. In some cases they have been rounded up or down and are therefore approximate.

WEIGHT

METRIC/IMPERIAL

7g	$^1/_4$ ounce	140g	5 ounces	600g	1 pound 5 ounces
20g	$^3/_4$ ounce	150g	$5^1/_2$ ounces	700g	1 pound 9 ounces
25–30g	1 ounce	175-180g	6 ounces	750g	1 pound 10 ounces
40g	$1^1/_2$ ounces	200g	7 ounces	800g	$1^3/_4$ pounds
50g	$1^3/_4$ ounces	220–225g	8 ounces	900g	2 pounds
60–65g	$2^1/_4$ ounces	250–260g	9 ounces	1kg	$2^1/_4$ pounds
70–75g	$2^1/_2$ ounces	300g	$10^1/_2$ ounces	1.2kg	$2^3/_4$ pounds
80g	$2^3/_4$ ounces	325g	$11^1/_2$ ounces	1.5kg	3 pounds 5 ounces
90g	$3^1/_4$ ounces	350g	12 ounces	2kg	$4^1/_2$ pounds
100g	$3^1/_2$ ounces	400g	14 ounces	2.5kg	$5^1/_2$ pounds
110–115g	4 ounces	450g	1 pound	3kg	$6^1/_2$ pounds
120–130g	$4^1/_2$ ounces	500g	1 pound 2 ounces		

VOLUME

METRIC/IMPERIAL

50ml	$1^3/_4$ fl oz		300ml	10 fl oz
60ml	2 fl oz (4 tablespoons/$^1/_4$ cup)		350ml	12 fl oz
75ml	$2^1/_2$ fl oz (5 tablespoons)		400ml	14 fl oz
90ml	3 fl oz ($^3/_8$ cup)		450ml	15 fl oz
100ml	$3^1/_2$ fl oz		475ml	16 fl oz (2 cups)
125ml	4 fl oz ($^1/_2$ cup)		500ml	18 fl oz
150ml	5 fl oz ($^2/_3$ cup)		600ml	20 fl oz
175ml	6 fl oz		800ml	28 fl oz
200ml	7 fl oz		850ml	30 fl oz
250ml	8 fl oz (1 cup)		1 litre	35 fl oz (4 cups)

LENGTH

METRIC/IMPERIAL

5mm	$\frac{1}{4}$ inch	5cm	2 inches	14cm	$5\frac{1}{2}$ inches
1cm	$\frac{1}{2}$ inch	6cm	$2\frac{1}{2}$ inches	20cm	8 inches
2cm	$\frac{3}{4}$ inch	8cm	$3\frac{1}{4}$ inches	24cm	$9\frac{1}{2}$ inches
2.5cm	1 inch	9cm	$3\frac{1}{2}$ inches	30cm	12 inches
3cm	$1\frac{1}{4}$ inches	10cm	4 inches		
4cm	$1\frac{1}{2}$ inches	12cm	$4\frac{1}{2}$ inches		

GLOSSARY

Below are the American terms for some of the ingredients and equipment used in this book.

arrowroot potato starch
aubergine eggplant
bacon rasher bacon slice
bain marie water bath
baking parchment wax paper
beef topside top, eye or bottom round of beef
beetroot beets
bicarbonate of soda baking soda
black cherries dark sweet cherries
black pudding blood sausage
broad beans fava beans
butterbeans lima beans
caster sugar superfine sugar
celeriac celery root
chicory Belgian endive
chips French fries
cling film plastic wrap
coriander cilantro (when referring to the green, leafy herb rather than the seeds)
cornflour cornstarch
courgette zucchini
double cream heavy cream
frying pan skillet
full-fat milk whole milk
gammon smoked ham
greaseproof paper parchment paper
grey mullet mullet, striped bass
grilled broiled

icing sugar confectioner's sugar
joint roast
loaf tin loaf pan
minced beef ground beef
monkfish anglerfish
mushy peas cooked dried marrowfat peas, simmered until they break up
pig's trotter pig's foot
plaice flounder, sole
plain chocolate semisweet chocolate
plain flour all-purpose flour
pork belly sparerib
prawns shrimp
red pepper red bell pepper
roasting tin roasting pan '
rocket arugula
sea bream snapper
sea trout steelhead trout
self-raising flour self-rising flour
shrimps very small shrimp
sieve strainer
single cream light cream
spring onion green onion
strong bread flour bread flour
swede rutabaga
tomato purée tomato paste
vanilla pod vanilla bean

Introduction

Going out for a good dinner has never been so accessible or affordable, thanks to a modern culinary sensation – the gastropub.

A gastropub is not just any old pub that serves food; it is much more than that. To qualify as a member of the dining phenomenon of the past decade, the surroundings, the atmosphere, the sounds, the aromas and, most importantly, the food needs to be spot on.

The term gastropub (not yet in the OED) was coined in the early Nineties to convey a style of eating out far removed from the formality of restaurant dining. The Eagle in Farringdon, set up by Mike Belben and David Eyre in 1991, was the forerunner. An old rough and tumble boozer, with an open kitchen, mismatched plates and battered institutional furniture, it set the blueprint for egalitarian dining. All comers were welcome to eat good, simple food, while enjoying a pint and a chat in the simple, unfussy 'public house' environment.

This winning formula has led to gastropubs opening up all over London and throughout the country. You could even argue that the gastropub has brought about a democratisation of the British dining culture. Its runaway success has demonstrated the missing link between the lively social environment of pubs and the more restrained atmosphere of fine dining. The point is that gastropubs are accessible: you should be able to just pop in and have a pint and a bite without any formality. Better still, instead of chicken in a basket or warmed-over frozen lasagne, you can enjoy a prime piece of Gloucester Old Spot and have a glass of Pinot Noir to accompany it.

However, not all so-called gastropubs are what they seem. With the steady rise in popularity of the independent gastropub came the big boys. Canny operators in the large breweries saw the success of the early operations and jumped on the bandwagon, creating chains of pseudo gastropubs. These pubs are fairly easy to identify, the telltale signs being the permanent chalk blackboards (no rubbing off there), the identikit well-worn furniture and a hackneyed, underwhelming menu.

Another interloper is 'the restaurant in disguise'. From the outside these joints may look like your friendly local but, on closer inspection, the high prices and bar not in the habit of serving pints show that they are really a restaurant behind the façade of a pub.

The term 'gastropub' itself is contentious. Coined in the mid-Nineties by a London listings magazine, it is a term that I, along with many other stalwarts, actually quite dislike. I share Mike Belben's views on the matter. Asked how best to describe the Eagle after it first opened, he said the best explanation was that it was 'simply a pub, it's what a pub should be'. I couldn't agree more. Nevertheless, the term makes an easy soundbite, and is a convenient pigeonhole into which to slot the new pubs.

The crucial element of a good gastropub is, of course, the food. While I don't expect to pay homage to every gastropub dish over the next two hundred-odd pages, I do hope to provide the tools to recreate in the comfort of your own kitchen all the best-known and emerging classics from this new British cuisine.

The relaxed nature of the pub environment is reflected in the classic gastropub menu. No room for the purist here, it's all about mixing and matching. Rustic French and Italian dishes can sit side by side with sturdy, old-fashioned British offerings. It is precisely this freedom that defines gastropub cookery.

All dishes are only ever as good as their raw ingredients, and gastropub chefs are great champions of local British produce. We are all becoming increasingly aware of the origins and the nature of production of our meat, fish, fruit and vegetables, and the ever-popular farmers' markets are making buying great ingredients easy and pleasurable. Supermarkets are now putting some effort in too, so shopping for the all-important raw produce has never been easier.

From the simplest bar food through to robust French and Italian main courses, topped off with a classic British pud, this book represents the food I enjoy eating and, more importantly, love to cook. I've stuck firmly to the simplicity of the gastropub menu and there isn't anything here that you can't make at home. Most of the dishes I've featured can be found on the blackboards of good gastropubs across the country. I've also included a few retro classics and some dishes that I cooked at the beginning of my career in the gastropubs of their time, the Sydney bistros. Oh, and I've borrowed recipes from some of my favourite places to eat: the Anchor and Hope, the Cat and Mutton, the Eagle....

Trish Hilferty
London, August 2006

Roast pumpkin

wild mushroom

clams, white

Smoked hadd

Cod & oysters

Soups

Leek and Potato Soup
Split Pea and Ham Soup
Watercress Soup
Lentil and Lemon Soup
White Bean Soup
Sweetcorn Chowder
Spring Minestrone
Pasta e Ceci
Chilled Tomato and Basil Soup
Potato and Wild Garlic Leaf Soup

Leek and Potato Soup

The secret of this simple soup lies in the slow sweating down of the vegetables, thyme and bay, which brings out the natural sugars of the leeks. More often than not, I leave the soup thick and chunky, making it a robust meal in itself with a wedge of crusty bread. However, it is easily poshed up with the addition of a little cream and a blitz in a blender.

SERVES 6

60g unsalted butter
6 leeks, sliced
1 onion, sliced
1 bay leaf
a sprig of thyme
1kg floury potatoes, such as King Edward or Maris Piper, peeled and diced
1.2 litres of water or light chicken stock
2 tablespoons snipped chives
3 tablespoons soured cream
sea salt and freshly ground black pepper

Melt the butter in a heavy-based saucepan and add the leeks, onion, bay, thyme and a pinch of sea salt. Cover and sweat over a low heat for 10–15 minutes, stirring from time to time, until the vegetables are soft.

Meanwhile, rinse the diced potatoes under the cold tap until the water is clear; this is to remove the starch, which could make the soup thick and gluey.

Add the potatoes to the pan and cover with the water or stock. Simmer until the potatoes are tender, then season with salt and pepper. At this point the soup is ready, though for a smoother version you could crush the potatoes with a potato masher or the back of a fork, or whiz the soup to a smooth purée in a blender.

Pour into warmed bowls and scatter with the snipped chives. Serve with a dollop of soured cream.

Split Pea and Ham Soup

Otherwise known as a 'London particular', after the thick pea-souper fogs that covered London in the nineteenth and early-twentieth centuries, this warm and hearty soup is as comforting as a favourite old jumper. Here I've given double quantities, as it is so moreish. One bowlful is never enough.

You can adjust the amount of liquid so as to make it as thick as you like, using green or yellow split peas or even adding fresh peas to lighten the soup in the spring.

SERVES 8–10

500g dried split peas
3 litres water
1 large onion, diced
2 carrots, diced
2 garlic cloves, crushed
1 smoked ham hock, weighing about 500g
1 bay leaf
a sprig of thyme
soured cream, to serve
sea salt and freshly ground black pepper

Wash the peas and put them in a large pot. Cover with the water, bring to the boil and skim off any scum from the surface. Now add the vegetables, garlic, ham hock and herbs and simmer for about 1$^1/_2$ hours, until the peas are tender. Remove the hock, throw away the skin and bones and shred the meat. At this stage you can purée the soup in a food processor or blender for a smoother texture, if you prefer.

Return the shredded ham to the soup and season with pepper and a little salt – remember that the smoked hock has quite a strong, salty flavour. Ladle the soup into warmed bowls, adding a small blob of soured cream to each one.

Watercress Soup

Here is a simple and versatile soup, delicious served either hot or cold.

A familiar addition to the salad bowl or used as a garnish alongside steak or game birds, the dark green leaves of watercress have a strong, peppery flavour that works beautifully with the soothing potato to make a fine first course.

SERVES 6

3 bunches of watercress
60g unsalted butter
2 onions, diced
1kg floury potatoes, such as King Edward or Maris Piper, peeled and diced
1.2 litres water or light chicken stock
6 tablespoons crème fraîche
sea salt and freshly ground black pepper

Cut the stalks off the watercress, discard the tough ends, then chop the rest finely. Melt the butter in a heavy-based saucepan and add the onions and watercress stalks. Cover and cook over a low heat until soft, stirring occasionally.

Meanwhile, rinse the diced potatoes under the cold tap until the water is clear; this is to remove the starch, which could make the soup thick and gluey. Add the potatoes to the pan, followed by the water or stock. Bring to a simmer and cook until the potatoes are soft.

Cool the soup a little, then liquidise in a blender, adding a handful of watercress leaves to each batch. Season with sea salt and a little freshly ground black pepper to taste. If you are serving the soup on a hot summer's day, leave it to chill in the fridge. Otherwise reheat gently and pour into warmed bowls. To finish the soup, either hot or cold, swirl in a dollop of crème fraîche.

Lentil and Lemon Soup

Lentil soup is one of the great staples of the pub menu – well, at least it is on mine. The lentil you use is up to you. I mostly choose Puy lentils – small, nutty, dark blueish ones from France – but brown, red or yellow lentils can be used instead. All lentils need a good wash before use, as they carry a little grit on them and can also contain the odd tiny surprise stone.

SERVES 4–6

2 tablespoons olive oil
1 onion, chopped
1 carrot, chopped
1 celery stalk, chopped
2 garlic cloves, chopped
200g lentils
1 litre water
a sprig of thyme
1 bay leaf
2 lemons
100ml extra virgin olive oil,
a small bunch of basil
sea salt and freshly ground black pepper

Heat the olive oil in a heavy-based pan and add the onion, carrot, celery, garlic and a pinch of sea salt. Cover and cook over a low heat for about 10 minutes, stirring occasionally, until the vegetables are soft. Add the lentils, water, thyme and bay and bring to the boil. Halve one of the lemons and squeeze the juice into the pan, adding the empty lemon halves too. Simmer for anything from 30 minutes to 1 hour. The cooking time will depend on the type of lentils you use: Puy lentils will take about 45 minutes and brown lentils 30–40 minutes, whereas red and yellow lentils will break down in around 20 minutes.

When the lentils are soft, remove the lemon halves, bay leaf and thyme. If you like a smooth soup, this is the time to liquidise it in a blender or simply squash it with a potato masher. Season with salt and pepper. Squeeze the juice from the remaining lemon into a small mixing bowl, then add a pinch each of salt and pepper and whisk in the extra virgin olive oil.

Pour the soup into warmed bowls and spoon a tablespoon or so of the lemon and oil mixture on top, followed by a generous sprinkling of torn basil leaves.

White Bean Soup

This is an incredibly simple and pure soup, allowing the sweetness of the beans to shine through. Go the extra mile and use good dried beans. Their flavour is far superior to the canned variety and the cooking liquid becomes the best-tasting vegetable stock available. Poured over thick slices of grilled country bread and topped with a punchy, green extra virgin olive oil, this soup makes a perfect lunch.

SERVES 4–6

350g dried cannellini beans
1 bay leaf
a sprig of thyme or rosemary
3 tablespoons olive oil
3 garlic cloves, chopped
2 onions, chopped
2 carrots, chopped
2 celery stalks, chopped
extra virgin olive oil
sea salt and freshly ground black pepper

Put the beans in a large bowl and add enough water to cover by at least 10cm. Leave to soak overnight.

When you are ready to make the soup, drain the beans and rinse them in cold water. Put them in a pot and pour in enough fresh water to cover them by 10cm. Bring to the boil, skim off any scum from the surface, then add the bay and thyme or rosemary. Turn the heat down low and simmer for 1–1$\frac{1}{2}$ hours, until the beans are soft. Season with a good pinch of sea salt and set them aside in their liquid.

Heat the oil in a large, heavy-based pan and add the garlic, onions, carrots, celery and a pinch of sea salt. Cover and cook over a low heat for 10–15 minutes, until the vegetables are soft and translucent. Add the cooked beans and their liquid and simmer for 10 minutes. Take out a cup of beans and purée them in a blender, then return them to the pot. Season the soup with salt and pepper to taste. Pour into warmed bowls and drizzle over some extra virgin olive oil.

Sweetcorn Chowder

I start making this soup at the end of summer, when the first sweetcorn hits the market. As autumn progresses, I tend to make it a bit thicker each time, either by reducing the liquid or substituting double cream for some of the milk. By all means leave the bacon out if you want a meatless soup, though I think the smokiness gives it more depth.

SERVES 6

50g unsalted butter
200g smoked streaky bacon, diced
1 onion, diced
2 celery stalks, diced
500g floury potatoes, such as King Edward or Maris Piper, peeled and diced
1 bay leaf
600ml light chicken stock
3 corn on the cob, the kernels carefully sliced off
500ml full-fat milk
1 tablespoon chopped parsley
sea salt and freshly ground black pepper

Melt the butter in a heavy-based saucepan, add the bacon and sauté until golden brown and crisp. Add the onion and celery, then cover and cook over a low heat for about 5 minutes, until they are soft and translucent. Add the potatoes, bay leaf and stock and cook over a medium heat for 15 minutes, until the potatoes are tender. Add the sweetcorn kernels and milk and simmer for 5–10 minutes, until the corn is cooked. Don't let the soup boil vigorously or it may curdle.

Season with sea salt and black pepper, ladle into warmed bowls and sprinkle with the parsley.

Spring Minestrone

This recipe and the one that follows are classic Italian soups. Both are rustic and hearty and fit squarely on pub blackboards. Minestrone is a thick vegetable soup that has as many versions as there are regions of Italy. It also changes with the seasons, so a spring *minestra* will include peas, broad beans and young artichokes alongside the staples of potatoes, onions, carrots and pasta.

SERVES 6–8

3 artichokes
juice of 1 lemon
100ml olive oil
3 garlic cloves, finely chopped
1 onion, diced
2 carrots, diced
1 large leek, diced
2 celery stalks, diced
2 medium-sized waxy potatoes, peeled and diced
150g shelled fresh peas
150g shelled fresh broad beans
400g canned cannellini beans, drained (or 200g dried beans, soaked and cooked as for
*   White Bean Soup, see page 17)*
150g tubular soup pasta, such as penne or ditaloni
freshly grated Parmesan cheese, to serve
extra virgin olive oil
sea salt and freshly ground black pepper

Trim the tough outer leaves off the artichokes, slice off the tops, then cut them in half lengthways and remove the hairy choke. Slice the artichokes into thin strips and put them in a bowl of fresh water with the lemon juice so they don't discolour.

Warm the olive oil in a heavy-based pan and add the garlic, onion, carrots, leek and celery. Cover and cook over a low heat for about 5 minutes. Add the potatoes and cook for 10 minutes. Now add the peas and broad beans, stirring to coat them in the oil. Pour in enough water to cover, then bring to a simmer and cook for 15–20 minutes, until the vegetables are tender. Drain the artichokes, add them to the pan and cook for 5 minutes.

Add the cannellini beans and pasta, then more water to cover again if it's needed, and cook over a medium heat until the pasta is done. Season with sea salt and pepper. Ladle into warmed bowls and serve with grated Parmesan and a splash of extra virgin olive oil.

Pasta e Ceci

This hearty soup is robust enough to be a meal in itself. It should be thick enough to stand a spoon in it. I make it in the Roman style, which is quite basic – just the chickpeas, tomatoes and loads of garlic, which becomes less intense through the long cooking time.

SERVES 6

300g dried chickpeas
4 bay leaves
3 tablespoons olive oil
10–12 garlic cloves, chopped
250g tomatoes, skinned and chopped
200g dried tagliatelle, broken into short lengths
freshly grated Parmesan cheese, to serve
extra virgin olive oil
sea salt and freshly ground black pepper

Put the chickpeas in a large bowl and add enough water to cover by at least 10cm. Leave to soak overnight.

The next day, drain the beans and rinse them under cold running water. Put them in a heavy-based saucepan or pasta pot with 2.5 litres of water and bring to the boil. Skim off any foamy scum that rises to the surface, add the bay leaves and 1 tablespoon of the olive oil, then lower the heat and simmer for 1¹/₂ hours.

Warm the rest of the olive oil in a pan and add the garlic. Cook over a low heat for about 5 minutes, stirring occasionally. Be sure not to let the garlic colour too much; it should be soft and translucent. Add the tomatoes and cook over a medium heat for 10 minutes. Stir the tomato mixture into the chickpeas and cook for a further hour.

Remove 3–4 ladlefuls of the soup, blitz in a blender or food processor, then return it to the pot. Add the tagliatelle and cook until it is *al dente*. Season with salt and pepper. Ladle the soup into warmed bowls, sprinkle with Parmesan and add a good glug of extra virgin olive oil.

Chilled Tomato and Basil Soup

I make many different kinds of tomato soup, depending on the seasons or simply what takes my fancy: thick and hearty *pappa al pomodoro* in the winter, or a 'cream of tomato' not unlike the Heinz variety I grew up with, and a gazpacho laced with fine sherry vinegar and good extra virgin olive oil in the summer. This Italian-influenced cold soup is simple and refreshing. I make it at the height of summer with the best ripe tomatoes I can find and finish it with a splash of extra virgin olive oil. It makes a perfect start to a summer dinner and is great for a light lunch on a baking hot day, accompanied by grilled garlicky sourdough bread.

SERVES 4

750g ripe tomatoes
2 garlic cloves
2 tablespoons red wine vinegar
3 tablespoons olive oil
1 teaspoon tomato purée
200ml water
2 tablespoons torn basil leaves
extra virgin olive oil
sea salt and freshly ground black pepper

Chop the tomatoes and garlic and place them in a bowl. Add the vinegar, olive oil and tomato purée and season with sea salt and pepper. Cover the bowl and chill for around an hour to marinate the tomatoes.

Transfer the mixture to a blender, add the water and liquidise at high speed for 2 minutes. Serve the soup in chilled bowls, sprinkled with the torn basil leaves and drizzled with a good glug of extra virgin olive oil.

Potato and Wild Garlic Leaf Soup

Wild garlic leaves, or ramsons, arrive with the first warm days of spring, around the end of March or beginning of April. The pretty white flowers with flat, dark green leaves grow in woodlands and alongside riverbanks and have a subtle garlic flavour. Like garlic, they are, surprisingly, a member of the lily family. The leaves and flowers can be chopped and added to salads, stir-fries and mashed potato, though they are also lovely wilted into this smooth and silky potato soup.

SERVES 4

50g unsalted butter
1 leek, finely sliced
1 onion, finely sliced
600g floury potatoes, such as King Edward or Maris Piper, peeled and diced
1 litre light chicken stock
a good handful of wild garlic leaves, chopped
sea salt and freshly ground black pepper

Melt the butter in a heavy-based saucepan and add the leek, onion and a small pinch of sea salt. Cover and cook for about 10 minutes, until the vegetables are soft. Meanwhile, rinse the potatoes under the cold tap until the water runs clear; this is to remove the starch, which could make the soup thick and gluey.

Add the potatoes to the pot, pour in the stock and cook over a medium heat for 15–20 minutes, until the potatoes are tender. Whiz the soup in a blender until smooth, then return to the pan and season with sea salt and black pepper.

Divide the chopped garlic leaves between 4 warmed bowls and ladle over the soup. The leaves will wilt in the heat of the soup.

Roast pumpkin

Wild mushroo

Clams, white

Smoked hadd

Cod & parsley

On Toast

Squid and Aioli
Chicken Livers and Bacon
Serrano Ham and Pan con Tomate
Pork and Rabbit Rillettes
Grilled Sardines and Tapenade
Crab on Toast
Welsh Rarebit
Scotch Woodcock
Devilled Kidneys
Black Pudding and Mushrooms
Snails, Bacon and Laverbread on Duck Fat Toast
Spinach, Anchovy and Soft-boiled Egg
Salt Cod Brandade

Squid and Aioli

The most important rule when cooking squid is not to overcook it, as it easily becomes tough and chewy. It's worth noting that after you remove the squid from the grill it will keep on cooking in its own heat. So give it just a few minutes on a hot grill or barbecue, then toss it with a sharp, lemony dressing for a quick and luscious snack.

SERVES 4

500g small squid, about 10–12cm long
115ml extra virgin olive oil
juice of 1 lemon
4 thick slices of sourdough bread
1 garlic clove, peeled
100g rocket leaves
Aioli (see page 231)
sea salt and freshly ground black pepper

To clean the squid, hold the body in one hand and the tentacles in the other, then pull and twist – the innards and tentacles will come away together. Cut the tentacles away just underneath the ink sac and squeeze out and discard the hard beak. Pull the purple membrane off the body and remove the quill from inside the body. Cut off and keep the wings. Wash the squid thoroughly under cold running water and drain.

Slit each body along one side and open it out. With a sharp knife, score the inside diagonally in each direction, giving a crisscross effect. Slice the body, wings and tentacles into bite-sized pieces, place in a bowl and toss with a tablespoon of the olive oil to coat. Season with sea salt and black pepper.

Whisk together the lemon juice and remaining olive oil in a large bowl and season with salt and pepper.

Cook the squid, in batches, on a barbecue or ridged grill pan over a medium-high heat for 1–2 minutes or until tender, turning it over half way through. Meanwhile, grill the bread and rub it with the garlic clove. Remove the squid from the grill and toss with the lemon and oil, then throw in the rocket and toss again.

Pile the squid and rocket on to the toast with a dollop of aioli.

Chicken Livers and Bacon

This makes a first-rate light supper. These humble offal morsels require a light touch and need to be cooked quickly, otherwise they can become dry and mealy.

SERVES 4

100g baby spinach leaves
2 tablespoons unsalted butter
4 streaky bacon rashers, cut into strips
300g chicken livers, trimmed of membrane
2 tablespoons sherry vinegar
4 thick slices of sourdough bread
sea salt and freshly ground black pepper

Wash and dry the spinach leaves, then place them in a wide bowl and set aside.

Heat the butter in a frying pan, add the bacon and fry for a minute or two over a medium heat, until it has released its fat and is becoming crisp. Remove from the pan and set aside. Add the chicken livers to the pan and sauté for 2–3 minutes, until brown and crisp on the outside but still pink in the middle. Season with sea salt and black pepper. Return the bacon to the pan and pour in the vinegar, scraping any crusty bits off the bottom of the pan with a wooden spoon to deglaze it. Pour the contents of the pan over the spinach leaves, tossing them as you go. The leaves will wilt a little in the heat of the livers. Toast the bread, then spoon the mixture on top and serve straight away.

Serrano Ham and Pan con Tomate

A Spanish-style bruschetta, pan con tomate is one of the many tapas dishes I picked up at the Eagle, whose food has a strong Iberian influence. Also known as *pan catalan*, it is simply thick slices of toast rubbed with garlic and a sweet ripe tomato and finished off with extra virgin olive oil. Any good cured ham will do, though I favour Serrano ham – delicious dark meat made from black Iberian pigs.

SERVES 4

4 thick slices of sourdough bread
2 garlic cloves, peeled
2 ripe tomatoes, halved
extra virgin olive oil
12 thin slices of Serrano ham
sea salt and freshly ground black pepper

Heat a ridged grill pan, then grill the bread on both sides. Rub the hot toast with a peeled garlic clove, then massage half a tomato into each slice. Season with sea salt and pepper, liberally douse with extra virgin olive oil and top each piece with 3 slices of ham.

Pork and Rabbit Rillettes

This is a classic French country dish, often found on charcuterie plates in bistros and restaurants around that country, and now frequently turning up as a starter in dining pubs in the UK. Rillettes consist of pork belly (and rabbit in this recipe) that has been slowly cooked in its own fat, cooled and shredded, then bound to a rough paste with the fat it was cooked in. This recipe may seem a bit hardcore and it is rather fatty, but I think of it as a treat – quite naughty but really tasty. It should be spread, thinly if you want, over crusty bread and served with cornichons.

SERVES 6–8

1kg rabbit forelegs
700g pork belly, boned, skinned and cut into 5cm cubes
1 bay leaf
a sprig of thyme
3 garlic cloves, crushed
200ml water
sea salt and freshly ground black pepper

Place the rabbit legs and pork in a bowl and rub them with a tablespoon of sea salt. Cover and refrigerate overnight.

The next day, preheat the oven to 140°C/275°F/Gas Mark 1. Put the meat in an ovenproof dish with the herbs, garlic, water and a grind of pepper. Cover the dish tightly, place in the oven and cook for $2^1/_2$–3 hours, until the meat is very tender. It shouldn't become dry or dark, so keep an eye on it and add more water if necessary.

Remove from the oven and leave until cool enough to handle easily. Pour the meat into a colander set over a bowl, reserving the fatty liquid and discarding the herbs. Strip the meat from the rabbit legs and place it in a bowl. Now add the pork and, with the aid of 2 forks, shred the meats together. It should be soft and stringy. Pour over enough of the fatty liquid to bind the meat together and season to taste.

Spoon the rillettes into a clean Kilner jar, where they will keep, covered with a layer of fat, for up to 6 months. Alternatively put them in a ceramic bowl or individual ramekins, cover and chill overnight – this way they will keep in the fridge for a week.

Grilled Sardines and Tapenade

My favourite version of sardines on toast, this makes a great outdoor lunch. Fresh sardines are unbeatable barbecue food. Their firm, oily flesh takes on a wonderful smokiness, they are quick and easy to cook and they sit perfectly with a piquant dressing such as tapenade.

I use a mortar and pestle for tapenade, as I like a rough, chunky texture. If you don't have one, a sturdy bowl and a rolling pin will give the same result. Only use a food processor at a push and if you do, crush the garlic first, then just pulse the mixture.

SERVES 6

24 sardines, scaled and gutted
extra virgin olive oil
6 thick slices of sourdough bread
lemon wedges, to serve
sea salt and freshly ground black pepper

For the tapenade
250g black olives, pitted
2 garlic cloves, peeled
30g capers
50g anchovies
1 teaspoon Dijon mustard
3 tablespoons olive oil
lemon juice

To make the tapenade, pound together the olives, garlic, capers and anchovies to a rough paste. Stir in the mustard, olive oil and a squeeze of lemon, then season to taste with sea salt and black pepper.

Heat a barbecue or ridged grill pan. Season the sardines with salt and pepper and rub them with a little olive oil. Carefully place the sardines on the grill and cook for about 2 minutes. Don't try to move them until they are coming away from the grill, then flip them over and cook for another minute or two. Transfer them to a warm plate.

Grill the bread on both sides, then douse each slice with extra virgin olive oil. Spread with some of the tapenade, top with the sardines and serve with lemon wedges.

Crab on Toast

A dollop of sweet crabmeat is probably the most luxurious thing you can have on toast. You could buy and cook live crabs for this dish but, as it's really just a snack, save yourself a little time and trouble and go with ready-picked crabmeat. Serve with a crisp salad.

SERVES 6

2 dressed crabs, weighing about 500g each in their shell
juice of ½ lemon
3 tablespoons olive oil
6 thick slices of sourdough bread
lemon wedges, to serve
sea salt and freshly ground black pepper

Pick the white crabmeat from the shell and put it into a bowl. Dig the brown meat from the sides of the shell and place it in another bowl. Season the white meat with a pinch of sea salt and a pinch of black pepper, then mix in the lemon juice and olive oil. Crush the brown meat with the back of a fork and season to taste.

Heat a ridged grill pan and grill the bread on both sides. Spread each slice of toast with the brown crabmeat, then top it off with the white. Serve with the lemon wedges.

Welsh Rarebit

The ideal bar snack. Quite simply, Welsh rarebit is super cheese on toast – and, it goes without saying, perfect with a pint.

Caerphilly, warmed with a real ale, is traditionally used for this dish, though there have always been regional variations, Lancashire, Cheshire and Gloucestershire being just three. These counties produce superb hard cheeses, which I often use as a base for this Welsh dish.

SERVES 4

50g unsalted butter
50g plain flour
1 teaspoon English mustard powder
300ml real ale or Guinness
350g Caerphilly cheese, grated
Tabasco and Worcestershire sauce
4 thick slices of white bread

Melt the butter in a heavy-based pan over a low heat. When it's just beginning to bubble, stir in the flour and mustard powder. Cook over a low heat for around a minute, until the mixture starts to brown slightly and give off a nutty aroma. Remove the pan from the heat and pour in the beer, whisking as you go to prevent it becoming lumpy. Return the pan to the hob and cook over a low heat for 10 minutes, until the sauce has thickened.

Add the cheese, along with a splash each of Tabasco and Worcestershire sauce, and let the cheese melt gently. Pour the mixture into a shallow container, press a layer of cling film on to the surface to prevent a skin forming, and leave it to cool for 5 minutes. This will set the mixture, making it pliable and easy to spread.

Preheat the grill and toast the bread on one side only. Spread a generous layer of rarebit on to the untoasted side and return it to the grill. Cook under the lowest possible heat until the cheese is bubbling and brown. Finish with an extra splash of Worcestershire sauce on the molten cheese.

Scotch Woodcock

Scotch woodcock was a popular savoury to finish off a meal in Victorian times. Often the recipe uses Gentlemen's Relish or an anchovy paste spread on the toast but I like to keep the anchovies whole, draped over the eggs.

SERVES 4

8 organic eggs
150ml double cream
40g unsalted butter
a pinch of cayenne pepper
1 tablespoon chopped parsley
4 thick slices of white bread
50g anchovy fillets
sea salt and freshly ground black pepper

Whisk the eggs and cream together with a pinch of sea salt and a grind of pepper. Melt the butter in a pan and add the egg mixture. Stir over a low heat until you have a creamy mass, then add the cayenne pepper and parsley and give it another quick mix.

Toast the bread and spoon the eggs on top. Cover with the anchovy fillets in a crisscross pattern.

Devilled Kidneys

Devilled kidneys aren't just for breakfast. They make a great light lunch or supper with the addition of sharp salad leaves such as watercress or dandelion.

This recipe serves 2. If you're doubling up, use 2 pans – the kidneys need to be cooked over a high heat so they don't stew and become tough.

SERVES 2

8 lamb's kidneys, skinned
100g plain flour
1 tablespoon English mustard powder
1 teaspoon cayenne pepper
50g unsalted butter
1 teaspoon olive oil
Tabasco and Worcestershire sauce
100ml chicken stock
2 thick slices of white bread
sea salt and freshly ground black pepper

Cut the kidneys in half lengthways. With a small knife, carefully cut out the white gristle from the middle of each one. In a bowl, mix together the flour, mustard powder and cayenne with a good pinch of salt and pepper, then throw in the kidneys, rolling them around to coat them in the seasoned flour.

Meanwhile, get a heavy-based frying pan hot and add the butter and oil. While it's getting to sizzling point, shake the excess flour from the kidneys. Throw them into the pan and cook over a high heat for a minute on each side, until they are browned, crisp and well sealed. Add a splash each of Tabasco and Worcestershire sauce and remove the kidneys from the pan. Pour the chicken stock into the pan, let it bubble, then reintroduce the kidneys. Heat through and check the seasoning. Toast the bread and serve the kidneys at once, on the hot toast, accompanied by a few sharp salad leaves.

Black Pudding and Mushrooms

This is a very popular starter or bar snack at the Fox in Shoreditch. It came about as an amalgamation of two salads at the suggestion of my sous chef, Sam Waterhouse. We tend to use morcilla for this dish; it's a spicier black pudding that gives a real depth of flavour.

SERVES 4

50g unsalted butter
1 garlic clove, finely chopped
500g large field mushrooms, sliced
1 teaspoon chopped parsley
1 tablespoon olive oil
200g morcilla sausage, sliced into rounds
4 thick slices of sourdough bread
sea salt and freshly ground black pepper

Melt the butter in a large pan, add the garlic with a pinch of sea salt and cook gently until soft. Tip in the mushrooms, add another pinch of salt and raise the heat to medium. Toss the mushrooms around in the garlicky butter.

Cover the pan, lower the heat and cook for 5 minutes or so, until the mushrooms are soft and have given up their juices, then season to taste. Stir in the parsley and set aside.

Heat the olive oil in a separate pan, add the morcilla and fry over a low heat for about 2 minutes, being careful not to break it up too much.

Toast the bread on both sides, then place on 4 plates. Spoon the mushrooms over each slice and top with the warm morcilla and serve immediately.

Snails, Bacon and Laverbread on Duck Fat Toast

This recipe comes from the country's leading gastropub, the redoubtable Anchor and Hope in London's Waterloo. I'll leave it in the capable hands of Jonathon Jones to explain his dish:

'I like this dish because it has so few ingredients, is simple to cook and yet packed full of flavour and texture. Also, while it smacks of traditional, gutsy French cooking – something we love – we actually make it with all British ingredients. We buy the laverbread from Wales, which your fishmonger may find for you, snails from Hereford and good smoked bacon from Essex.'

SERVES 2

4 thick rashers of smoked streaky bacon, cut into sticks
2 shallots, finely sliced
2 garlic cloves, crushed
20 cooked snails, out of their shells (available in cans in good delis)
a splash of white wine
2 tablespoons laverbread
80ml chicken stock
a handful of flat-leaf parsley, chopped
2 slices of good day-old bread, toasted and then smeared with duck fat
1/2 lemon
freshly ground black pepper

Set a heavy-based saucepan or casserole over a low heat, put in the bacon and stir. It will gently render its fat and start to brown and crisp up. When it has, add the shallots and garlic and stew gently until soft. Add the snails and stir to coat them in the fat. Now turn up the heat, add the white wine and boil until completely evaporated; the acidity of the wine will cut through the bacon fat. Turn the heat back down, stir in the laverbread and allow to stew for a few minutes. Add the chicken stock and bring it quickly back to the boil, stirring to prevent sticking. Tip in the parsley and taste for seasoning – it will be salty enough from the bacon and have a taste of the sea from the laverbread, so you'll probably need a grind of pepper only.

Pour the mixture over the warm duck fat toast and serve with a wedge of lemon for that extra zing.

Spinach, Anchovy and Soft-boiled Egg

Spinach and eggs have a natural affinity. The steeliness of the former balances the rich creaminess of a soft and gooey egg yolk. So it's not surprising that the two are paired together in many Italian dishes – think of the classic Florentine pizza. The anchovies here lend an extra dimension to this spin on a bruschetta, a final savoury, salty kick.

SERVES 4

4 organic eggs
1kg fresh spinach
2 tablespoons olive oil
1 garlic clove, finely chopped
juice of ½ lemon
4 thick slices of sourdough bread
extra virgin olive oil
12 anchovy fillets
sea salt and freshly ground black pepper

Bring a pan of water to the boil, add a small pinch of sea salt and carefully put the eggs in. Boil the eggs for 6 minutes, then remove from the pan and refresh under cold running water. When they are cool, peel the eggs and set aside.

Wash the spinach and remove the thick stalks, then spin it or shake it dry. Heat the olive oil in a large frying pan or wok and add the garlic. Cook until golden, then add the spinach and toss until it starts to wilt. Season with sea salt and pepper and the lemon juice.

Meanwhile, toast the bread under a hot grill. When it's ready, douse it with extra virgin olive oil.

Divide the toast between 4 plates and top with the spinach. Halve the eggs, sprinkle each half with a little black pepper and place on top of the spinach. Drape the anchovies over the eggs and serve at once.

Salt Cod Brandade

It would be remiss of me to have a toast section in this book without including a recipe for this pungent Provençal dish. Spread thickly on great slabs of sourdough toast, this light and fluffy purée makes a great snack with a few olives on the side, or the start to a memorable meal.

SERVES 6

700g salt cod
400g waxy potatoes, peeled and cut into chunks
3 garlic cloves, crushed
225ml warm milk
225ml warm extra virgin olive oil, plus a little extra for drizzling
juice of 1 lemon
4 thick slices of sourdough bread
sea salt and freshly ground black pepper

Cover the salt cod generously with cold water and leave to soak for 12 hours or overnight, changing the water several times.

Put the potatoes in a pan of water with a small pinch of sea salt and bring to the boil. Reduce the heat to medium and simmer gently until the potatoes are tender. Drain well, mash and keep warm.

While this is going on, drain the salt cod, put it in a pan with fresh, unsalted water and place it over a high heat. Just as the water begins to boil, remove the pan from the heat and leave to the side for 5 minutes so the cod poaches in the lingering heat. Remove the fish from the pan with a slotted spoon and leave it to cool on a plate. When it is cool enough to handle, peel off the skin and remove any bones. Flake the fish into the mashed potato and add the garlic.

Gradually add the warm milk and olive oil alternately to the mash, beating both in well until you have a light but slightly textured purée. Add lemon juice to taste, along with a good grind of black pepper and maybe a touch more salt if necessary.

Toast the bread. Spread the brandade on the toast and drizzle with a little extra virgin olive oil.

BRUNCH
AT WEEKENDS

REAL ALES
& GUEST BEERS

RIVERSIDE
TERR

Roast pumpkin

wild mushroo

Clams, white

Smoked hadd

Cod & stacker

Starters

Pork and Chicken Liver Terrine
Pig's Trotter Brawn
Ham and Parsley Terrine
Smoked Mackerel Pâté
Smoked Herring, Cucumber and Dill
Potted Shrimps
Beetroot and Horseradish
Mushrooms à la Greque with Green Beans and Rocket
Whelk Mayonnaise
Roast Pumpkin, Red Onion and Rocket
Waldorf Salad
Feta, Watermelon and Olives
Caesar Salad
Spiced Aubergine and Flatbread

Pork and Chicken Liver Terrine

How many times have you seen a country-style terrine in a deli and thought how difficult and time consuming it must be to make? Actually, it's not at all tricky, in fact it's really quick and easy to put together and will be ready the next day for a picnic, lunch or a dinner-party starter.

SERVES 10

1 small onion, finely diced
200ml red wine
10 rashers of rindless smoked streaky bacon
750g pork belly, coarsely minced
200g chicken livers, trimmed
50g pistachio nuts, lightly roasted
1 garlic clove, finely chopped
3 tablespoons brandy or Madeira
1 teaspoon thyme leaves
sea salt and freshly ground black pepper

Preheat the oven to 160°C/325°F/Gas Mark 3. Put the diced onion in a small saucepan and pour over the red wine. Place the pan over a low heat and simmer until all the wine has evaporated and the flavour has been absorbed. Remove from the heat and leave to cool.

Use the bacon rashers to line a terrine dish or loaf tin, 1–1.2 litres in capacity, arranging them crossways so that the edges are hanging over the sides. Put all the remaining ingredients, including the cooled onion, in a large bowl and mix really well. I squish it all together with my hands – this slightly breaks up the livers, which I think holds it all together a little better. Season with sea salt – don't be shy with this, it will take about 15g – and black pepper.

Squash the mixture into the lined terrine, fold over the hanging ends of bacon and cover with a lid or foil. Place the terrine in a roasting tin of hot water, filled to half way up the sides. Bake for 1–1½ hours. To test whether the terrine is cooked, pierce it with a skewer; it should come out hot and the juices should run clear. Let the terrine cool for 10 minutes, then weight it down, ideally with another loaf tin filled with food cans. Leave until the terrine is cool before you remove the weights, then refrigerate overnight.

To serve, turn the terrine out of the tin, cut it into thick slices with a sharp knife and eat it with crusty bread or sourdough toast and a dollop of fruit chutney, preferably Green Tomato Chutney or Rhubarb Chutney (see page 196).

Pig's Trotter Brawn

Brawn is part of classic charcuterie, known in French as *fromage de tête* or by the unattractive American name, 'head cheese'. As those names suggest, it is generally made with a whole pig's head, simmered until it falls away from the bones. As pig's heads are a bit tricky to come by, from time to time I make it with trotters and a ham hock for extra meaty content.

SERVES 8

4 pig's trotters
2 ham hocks
2 carrots, peeled
1 onion, peeled and halved
1 leek, halved
2 bay leaves
a sprig of thyme
10 black peppercorns
2 tablespoons white wine vinegar
1 tablespoon chopped tarragon
2 tablespoons chopped parsley
sea salt and freshly ground black pepper

Put the trotters and hocks into a large pan, cover with water and add the vegetables, bay, thyme, peppercorns, vinegar and a good pinch of sea salt. Bring to the boil, skim off any foamy scum from the surface, then cover the pot and simmer over a low heat for 2 hours, until the meat is tender and falling off the bones. Leave the meat to cool in the liquid.

Remove the trotters and ham hock from the pan and begin to pick off the meat – be careful, there are lots of tiny bones in the trotters, particularly on the hoof. Tip all the flesh on to a board and chop it roughly into small chunks, then place it in a large bowl with the tarragon and parsley. Taste and add a little salt and pepper, if necessary.

Strain the cooking liquor into a clean pan and boil it down. It should be concentrated but not too salty, so keep checking the flavour. Leave to cool.

Ladle some of the stock into the bowl and mix around to coat the meat, then check the seasoning – you may like a touch more vinegar to sharpen it. Pour the meat into a terrine mould or loaf tin, 1–1.2 litres in capacity, and ladle over enough stock to cover it by a fingernail depth. Cover and refrigerate overnight.

To serve, turn the terrine out of the tin, cut it into 1cm slices with a sharp knife and pass around cornichons and crusty country bread.

Ham and Parsley Terrine

This recipe is not a million miles away from the brawn, above, though it will probably appeal to the more fainthearted among you. You have the choice of using smoked or green hocks, or even a piece of gammon, which is what I often use when I have any left over.

SERVES 8

4 ham hocks
1 onion, peeled and quartered
2 carrots, peeled and cut in half
2 celery stalks, cut in half
2 bay leaves
1 tablespoon white wine vinegar
a bunch of parsley, preferably curly, chopped
1 tablespoon chopped tarragon
2 tablespoons capers, chopped
sea salt and freshly ground black pepper

Place the ham hocks in a large pan and cover with cold water. Add the onion, carrots, celery, bay and vinegar and bring to a simmer over a medium to high heat. Cover the pot, reduce the heat to low and simmer for 2–2$\frac{1}{2}$ hours, until the hocks are tender and the meat is beginning to fall off the bone. Remove the hocks and set aside to cool a little. Strain the liquid into a clean pan and boil until reduced by a third or so; you need to keep tasting the liquor so it doesn't become too strong or sharp from the vinegar. Take it off the heat and leave to cool.

When the hocks are cool enough to handle, remove the meat from the bone, set it on a board and chop it into 1cm chunks. Put them in a bowl, mix in the parsley, tarragon and capers, then add a little seasoning if necessary. Pour over enough liquid just to pull it all together.

Pour the mixture into a terrine mould or loaf tin, 1–1.2 litres in capacity, and press it all down firmly. Pour over any remaining liquid to cover it by a fingernail depth. Cover and chill overnight.

To serve the terrine, turn it out on to a board and cut it into 1cm slices with a sharp knife. Accompany with a simple salad of finely sliced shallots and parsley, dressed with a touch of red wine vinegar and olive oil, and a crusty baguette.

Smoked Mackerel Pâté

I suppose this recipe is more of a paste than a pâté, reminiscent of those fishy spreads you can find in tiny jars in supermarkets. It's so much nicer, though, and ever so simple to make. Blending the smoky fish with lots of butter gives the pâté a smooth, luxurious texture and flavour.

SERVES 6

500g smoked mackerel fillets
250g unsalted butter, softened
juice of 1 lemon
lemon wedges, to serve
freshly ground black pepper

Peel the skin off the mackerel fillets, pick out any bones and place the flesh in a food processor with the softened butter. Whiz for 2 minutes or until the fish and butter are completely amalgamated and you have a smooth paste. Squeeze in the lemon juice and a grind of black pepper and give the mixture another quick burst. Scrape the paste out into a dish, cover and chill for about an hour. Serve with the lemon wedges and some hot rye toast.

Smoked Herring, Cucumber and Dill

This is a light and uncomplicated salad, though one I find complex in flavour. It's a pleasing blend of smoky fish and sharp mustard dressing, with the crunch of the vegetables and slightly aniseedy flavour of the dill.

SERVES 4–6

1 cucumber
$1/2$ teaspoon sea salt
$1/2$ teaspoon caster sugar
200g green beans, trimmed
500g smoked herring fillets
a small bunch of dill

For the dressing
1 tablespoon Dijon mustard
$1/2$ teaspoon caster sugar
4 teaspoons white wine vinegar
4 tablespoons olive oil
freshly ground black pepper

Peel the cucumber, slice it in half lengthways and, with the aid of a teaspoon, dig out the seeds. Cut the cucumber across into slices 1cm thick and place them in a colander. Sprinkle over the sea salt and sugar and shake around to coat all the pieces. Place the colander over a bowl and leave for half an hour to extract some of the liquid.

Cook the green beans in boiling salted water until tender, then drain. Plunge them into cold water to cool them quickly so they keep their colour and crunch, then drain again.

Meanwhile, make the dressing. Combine the mustard, sugar and vinegar in a bowl and stir until the sugar has dissolved. Add the oil in a slow, steady stream, mixing all the time, until it has completely emulsified. Season with a grind of black pepper.

Peel any skin off the herring fillets and slice them into 1cm strips. Gently squeeze any liquid from the cucumber strips and dry them on kitchen paper or a tea towel. Also dry off any remaining water from the beans.

Combine the fish, cucumber and beans in a bowl. Strip the dill fronds from their stalks, chop them roughly and add to the bowl. Toss gently with enough dressing to coat.

Potted Shrimps

I've always loved potted shrimps. What's not to love about fresh shrimps bound together in a load of butter? Though I do remember that when I first started making them in restaurants I was only ever supplied with whole brown shrimps and had to peel millions of them to get enough to last a lunchtime. Nightmare! Luckily it's now easy to find peeled shrimps. If you do have any trouble laying your hands on them, chopped fresh prawns make a fine substitute.

SERVES 6

150g unsalted butter
2 blades of mace
a pinch of cayenne pepper
500g peeled brown shrimps
a squeeze of lemon
lemon wedges, to serve
sea salt and freshly ground black pepper

Put the butter in a pan with the mace and cayenne pepper and melt over a low heat. Now add the shrimps and heat through for a couple of minutes on a low flame; don't let them boil, as they can become tough and rubbery. Add a squeeze or two of lemon juice, then season with a little sea salt and a grind of pepper. Remove the mace blades and spoon the shrimps and butter into 6 small ramekins, pressing the mixture down to give a level surface. Cover and chill for at least an hour. Serve with lemon wedges and some hot toast.

Beetroot and Horseradish

Although I have a penchant for pickled beetroot from a jar and use it often at home, this recipe is infinitely better if you cook your own beetroot. Apart from the standard purple beets, which are on offer all year round, the summer months bring golden beetroot, cylindrical red beets and 'heritage', globe-shaped beets with red and white striped flesh. Oh, and don't throw away the leaves, they are delicious.

Serve this as a starter, on its own for a light lunch, or as a side dish with steak, game or fish.

SERVES 6

1kg fresh beetroot, with leaves attached
250ml water
1 tablespoon red wine vinegar
1 tablespoon olive oil
sea salt and freshly ground black pepper

For the horseradish cream
2cm stick of fresh horseradish
a squeeze of lemon juice
1 teaspoon Dijon mustard
250ml crème fraîche

Preheat the oven to 180°C/350°F/Gas Mark 4. Cut the leafy stems off the beetroot and soak them in cold water to revive them. Wash the beets but don't peel them or the colour will run. Place the beets in a baking tin and add the water, vinegar, oil and a good pinch of sea salt. Cover with foil and bake for 1 hour or until you can easily pierce the beetroot with a skewer. Leave until cool enough to handle, then peel or rub the skins off. This job is best done wearing rubber gloves, as it's pretty messy.

Bring a pot of salted water to the boil, add the beetroot stems and boil for 2 minutes, until tender. Drain and set aside.

Meanwhile, make the horseradish cream. Peel the horseradish stick and grate it on the finest part of the grater into a bowl. Mix in the lemon juice, mustard and crème fraîche and season with sea salt and pepper to taste.

Slice the beets into quarters, chop the stems, then add them both to the bowl of horseradish cream. Mix together and check the seasoning again. Serve immediately.

Mushrooms à la Greque with Green Beans and Rocket

As the name suggests, *à la greque* refers to stewing vegetables in the Greek style, with fruity olive oil, lemon and the gentle spice of coriander seeds. Mushrooms in particular absorb these flavours beautifully. It also works well with leeks, fennel, young courgettes or artichokes – you only need to amend the cooking time. To add a little extra oomph to this salad, you could finish it with a crumbling of Feta cheese.

SERVES 6

1 tablespoon coriander seeds
1 lemon
200ml water
120ml olive oil
2 garlic cloves, lightly crushed
1 bay leaf
a sprig of thyme
500g button mushrooms
200g green beans
200g rocket
sea salt and freshly ground black pepper

Roast the coriander seeds in a dry frying pan over a low heat for 1–2 minutes, until they are fragrant. Pare 2 or 3 strips of zest off the lemon with a vegetable peeler and put them in a pan. Squeeze in the lemon juice, then add the water, olive oil, garlic, herbs and the toasted seeds. Bring to the boil, season with a good pinch of sea salt and a grind of pepper and add the mushrooms. Cover, turn the heat down low and simmer for 10 minutes, until the mushrooms are tender. Remove from the heat and leave to cool.

Cook the green beans in boiling salted water until tender, then drain. Plunge them into cold water to cool them quickly so they keep their colour and crunch, then drain again.

At this point the mushrooms will be floating on top of the cooking liquid. Scoop them out with a slotted spoon into a salad bowl, then carefully spoon the oil off the top of the liquid and add it to the mushrooms; this will be your dressing.

Add the beans and rocket and toss gently to combine. Serve immediately, with crusty country bread.

Whelk Mayonnaise

I think the closest most whelks get to the pub is when they are pickled and sold from a seafood van outside. They are a greatly underappreciated mollusc – perhaps because they can be tough and rubbery, especially when cold. Still warm from the pot, though, and mixed with home-made mayo, whelks are a wonderful thing.

SERVES 4

1kg whelks
juice of $\frac{1}{2}$ lemon
1 tablespoon chopped parsley
1 tablespoon chopped chives
sea salt and freshly ground black pepper
1 quantity of Mayonnaise (see page 230)

Bring a large pot of salted water to the boil and carefully lower in the whelks. When the water has come back to the boil, simmer for 5 minutes and then drain.

To remove the whelks from their shells, first pull off the hard, flat disc (their foot), then prise out the flesh with a fork. Cut the dark sac from the end of the body and discard – this is the whelk's stomach. Chop the flesh roughly and place in a bowl with the lemon juice, herbs and mayonnaise. Mix everything together and season with black pepper and maybe just a little sea salt. Serve with freshly buttered baguettes.

Roast Pumpkin, Red Onion and Rocket

This is a wonderful autumnal salad, rich in colour and sweet from the long, slow roasting of the vegetables. When buying pumpkins, it's best to choose a small, firm fruit that feels heavy for its size. Larger pumpkins, particularly the round ones used for making Halloween lanterns, tend to have a high water content and collapse in the oven. The Crown Prince is my favourite variety. It has a greenish, blue-ridged skin and dense, bright-orange flesh that holds together well when roasted. Butternut squash makes a good year-round alternative.

SERVES 6

4 red onions
3 garlic cloves, lightly crushed
2 sprigs of thyme
1 tablespoon red wine vinegar
100ml olive oil
1 small pumpkin, weighing around 1.5kg
200g rocket
a chunk of Parmesan or Pecorino cheese, weighing about 100g
sea salt and freshly ground black pepper

For the dressing
4 teaspoons lemon juice
4 tablespoons extra virgin olive oil

Preheat the oven to 160°C/325°F/Gas Mark 3. Peel the red onions, making sure to keep the root intact, and cut them into quarters. Put them in a roasting tin with the garlic, thyme, vinegar and olive oil, place them on the hob over a medium heat and sauté for 2 minutes. Season with sea salt and black pepper, cover the tin with foil and bake in the oven for 40 minutes, until the onions are soft.

Meanwhile, cut the pumpkin in half and scoop out the seeds. Carefully slice it into crescent shapes and peel if you want to, though I love the earthy flavour of roasted skin. Toss the slices in a little olive oil and spread them out in a roasting tin. Bake in the oven for 40 minutes, until tender. Remove the onions and pumpkin from the oven and leave to cool slightly.

For the dressing, mix together the lemon juice and olive oil and season with a pinch of sea salt and a grind of pepper. Combine the rocket with the roasted vegetables and toss lightly with the dressing. Put everything on to a large platter and, using a vegetable peeler, shave the cheese over the top. Serve at once.

Waldorf Salad

I am never able to think of Waldorf salad without it conjuring up the memory of Basil Fawlty trying to explain to his American customers that they were 'fresh out of waldorfs', then shouting the ingredients to a mystified Manuel: 'Apples, celery, walnuts and grapes!' Comedy aside, this is actually a delicious autumnal salad. It's best made just as you are ready to serve, to retain the colour and crispness of the apples and nuts.

SERVES 4

4 apples, cored and cut into 2cm cubes
2 celery stalks, finely sliced
50g walnuts
2 Little Gem lettuces

For the dressing
2 organic egg yolks
1 teaspoon Dijon mustard
1 teaspoon lemon juice
200ml vegetable oil
a pinch of sea salt

First make the dressing. Put the egg yolks, mustard and lemon juice in a food processor and blend until well combined. With the machine running, gradually add the oil in a thin, steady stream until it has all been incorporated. If it is too thick, add a little warm water to thin it down. Season with sea salt and adjust the acidity with a little more lemon juice to taste, if necessary.

Combine the apples, celery and nuts in a bowl and add enough dressing just to hold them all together. Tear the lettuces into bite-sized pieces and mix them into the salad. Toss to coat with the dressing and serve immediately.

Feta, Watermelon and Olives

This is more of an instruction than a recipe and makes a perfect starter for the height of summer. As with most dishes this simple, it's important to use the best ingredients you can lay your hands on.

SERVES 6

1.5kg ripe watermelon
250g good Greek or Turkish Feta cheese
1 tablespoon lemon juice
3 tablespoons olive oil
200g rocket
100g black olives, preferably kalamata, pitted
sea salt and freshly ground black pepper

Peel the watermelon, taking care not to leave on any of the white rind. Cut it into chunks of about 4cm, removing the pips as you go. Slice the Feta into 4cm chunks, too.

Mix together the lemon juice and olive oil with a pinch of sea salt and a grind of pepper. Place the rocket in a bowl and dress lightly with the lemony olive oil, then add the watermelon, Feta and olives. Toss very gently so as not to break the pieces. Turn out on to a large platter to serve.

Caesar Salad

A small variation on Caesar Cardin's classic recipe, this is a Caesar salad my way. Although the ingredients are more or less the same as in the original, the method is quite different. Instead of using coddled or lightly cooked eggs as the base of the dressing, I like to serve them soft boiled on top of the salad. And instead of employing the faintly fishy flavour of Worcestershire sauce, I make a batch of my favourite anchovy dressing to coat the leaves.

SERVES 6

100g day-old white bread, cut into 1cm cubes
1 garlic clove, lightly crushed
2 tablespoons olive oil
6 organic eggs
2 Cos lettuces
a chunk of Parmesan cheese, weighing about 80–100g
a few good spoonfuls of Anchoïade (see page 231)
sea salt

Preheat the oven to 180°C/350°F/Gas Mark 4. Place the cubes of bread in a bowl with the garlic, olive oil and a pinch of sea salt and rub them together so the bread gets an even coating of oil. Put them on a baking tray and into the oven to cook for 10 minutes, until they are golden brown and crisp. Leave to cool.

Bring a pan of water to the boil, carefully add the eggs and cook for 6 minutes; they will be soft boiled and slightly runny. Cool immediately under cold running water and peel as soon as possible; the shell will come off easier that way.

To assemble the salad, tear up the larger lettuce leaves, leaving the smaller ones at the heart intact, and put them in a large salad bowl. Throw in the croûtons. Shave the Parmesan with a vegetable peeler and add to the bowl. Add a few good spoonfuls of the anchoïade and mix thoroughly. Distribute the salad between 6 plates and top each with a halved soft-boiled egg.

Spiced Aubergine and Flatbread

This dish is a very popular starter or bar snack at the Fox. The vegetables are stewed in the Mediterranean style, not unlike ratatouille, then lightly spiced with our home-made harissa. As with ratatouille, it's important that the components are cooked separately and when combined, left to cool for the flavours to amalgamate. The dish is finished off with a topping of crème fraîche, tahini or Feta cheese.

The quantities given below for the harissa make a fairly large batch but it will keep in the fridge, covered with a layer of oil and sealed, for up to a month.

SERVES 6

4 ripe tomatoes, cut into 1cm dice
200ml extra virgin olive oil
2 red onions, cut into 2cm dice
2 garlic cloves, chopped
3 large aubergines, cut into 2cm dice
crème fraîche, seasoned with salt and pepper, to serve
sea salt and freshly ground black pepper

For the flatbread
7g sachet of dried yeast
1 teaspoon sugar
90ml olive oil
570ml warm water
750g strong bread flour
2 teaspoons sea salt

For the harissa
1 teaspoon cumin seeds
10 garlic cloves, peeled
6 long red chillies, halved and seeded
1 teaspoon dried mint
1 teaspoon sea salt
1 bunch of coriander
1 bunch of mint
olive oil
juice of 1/2 lemon

The first step is to make the flatbread. Mix the yeast, sugar and olive oil with the water and leave to stand for a few minutes until the yeast starts to bubble on top. Sift the flour and salt into a food processor or an electric mixer fitted with a dough hook. Slowly pour in the liquid and mix until the dough forms a ball. If it seems a little dry, add a little warm water; conversely if it's too wet, add flour by the spoonful until it is smooth and elastic. Grease a bowl with olive oil and transfer the dough to it. Cover with a cloth and leave to rise in a warm place, until doubled in size.

For the harissa, dry roast the cumin seeds in a small frying pan over a low heat until they begin to pop and are fragrant. Put them in a food processor with the garlic, chillies, dried mint, salt and fresh herbs. I use all the coriander, leaves and stems, but discard the hard stems from the mint; the softer stems will purée well. Whiz on the highest speed, adding enough olive oil to make a smooth purée, then squeeze in the lemon juice.

Put the diced tomatoes into a large bowl with 3 tablespoons of the olive oil, a pinch of sea salt and a grind of black pepper and leave to marinate while you get on with cooking the rest of the vegetables. Heat 3 tablespoons of the remaining olive oil in a large, heavy-based frying pan and add the onions with a pinch of sea salt. Cover and cook over a low heat for 10 minutes, until they are soft and translucent, then add the garlic. Cook for a further 5 minutes. Remove with a slotted spoon and transfer to the bowl with the tomatoes.

Turn up the heat to medium, add another 3 tablespoons or so of oil to the pan and introduce half of the aubergines. Sauté for 5 minutes, stirring all the time, then reduce the heat to low and stew for 5–10 minutes, until they are soft. Add to the bowl and repeat with the remaining olive oil and aubergines. Mix in 1–2 tablespoons of harissa, to taste, then leave to cool.

To make the flatbreads, preheat a griddle pan or a flat, heavy-based frying pan – it needs to be completely free of oil as the high frying temperature could cause it to burn. Divide the dough into 6 balls and roll each one out on a floured surface to 5mm thick. Put 1 or 2 at a time in the hot pan and cook over a high heat until they bubble slightly and become golden underneath. Flip the breads over to cook the other side. Keep them warm while cooking the rest of the breads.

To serve, divide the flatbreads between 6 plates, add a mound of aubergine and top with a dollop of seasoned crème fraîche.

Roast pumpkin

wild mushroo

Clams, white

Smoked hadd

Cod & parsley

Pasta and Risotto

Crab Linguine
Penne with Sausage, Tomato and Sage
Pappardelle with Peas and Broad Beans
Rabbit Lasagne
Pumpkin and Ricotta Gnocchi
Wild Mushroom Risotto
Cavolo Nero Risotto
Shellfish Risotto

Crab Linguine

This simple pasta dish makes a wonderful summer lunch with a crisp green salad and a glass of dry white wine. I think it's important to use dried pasta here. Fresh pasta just doesn't have the same bite and I really enjoy the contrast between the *al dente* pasta and the soft, sweet crabmeat.

SERVES 4

100ml extra virgin olive oil
1 garlic clove, finely chopped
1 small red chilli, seeded and finely chopped
1 lemon
400g fresh crabmeat
400g dried linguine
2 tablespoons chopped parsley
sea salt and freshly ground black pepper

Warm the olive oil in a heavy-based saucepan and add the garlic and chilli. Cook over a low heat for 1–2 minutes, until they are just soft. Grate the zest of half the lemon, then squeeze the juice and add both to the pan along with the crabmeat. Stir to combine and heat gently until the crab is warmed through. Season with a grind of pepper and just a little sea salt.

Meanwhile, bring a large pot of salted water to a rolling boil and add the linguine. Give it a good stir and cook until *al dente*. Drain, then add to the warmed crabmeat, reserving a touch of the cooking water to help lubricate the sauce. Stir through the parsley and serve immediately.

Penne with Sausage, Tomato and Sage

This is the kind of simple pasta dish to make if you have only a few sausages in the fridge – not quite enough to stretch to a full meal but just enough to make a rustic sauce. I like to use a sausage with a bit of a kick, such as Italian pork and fennel. If I find I have only pork, or pork and leek sausages, I add a teaspoon or so of fennel seeds and a few flakes of chilli.

SERVES 4

3 tablespoons olive oil
1 onion, finely diced
2 garlic cloves, chopped
6 good-quality pork and fennel sausages
400g can of plum tomatoes
12 sage leaves, finely sliced
400g penne
freshly grated Parmesan cheese, to serve
sea salt and freshly ground black pepper

Heat the olive oil in a heavy-based saucepan, add the onion, garlic and a pinch of sea salt and cook over a low heat until soft and translucent. Peel the casing from the sausages and lightly crumble the meat into the pan. Raise the heat to medium and cook for about 5 minutes, stirring often, until the meat is lightly browned and cooked through. Add the tomatoes and simmer over a low heat for 20 minutes or until the sauce has thickened. Add the sage leaves and cook for a minute or two, so the sauce fully absorbs their flavour. Season with sea salt and black pepper.

Bring a large pot of salted water to a rolling boil and throw in the pasta. Stir once or twice to prevent it falling to the bottom and sticking. Cook until *al dente*, then drain and mix with the sauce. Serve in warmed deep bowls and pass around some freshly grated Parmesan.

Pappardelle with Peas and Broad Beans

Here we have the first pasta dish of spring and therefore probably my favourite. It's a joy to see fresh peas and broad beans after a winter that seems to have gone on forever (can you tell I'm writing this at the end of March?). However, if you feel you need a ray of winter sunshine, these are the two vegetables that can taste almost as good as the real thing after being frozen.

SERVES 4

50g unsalted butter
1 tablespoon olive oil
1 small onion, finely diced
200g shelled fresh peas, or frozen peas
200g shelled fresh broad beans, or frozen broad beans
200ml light chicken stock or water
100ml double cream
400g pappardelle
100g Parmesan cheese, freshly grated
sea salt and freshly ground black pepper

Melt the butter with the olive oil in a heavy-based saucepan over a medium heat. Add the onion with a pinch of sea salt, then cover and cook over a low heat for about 5 minutes, until soft and translucent. Add the peas and broad beans, plus the stock or water, and bring to a simmer. Cook over a low heat for 10 minutes, until the vegetables are tender and have absorbed most of the liquid. Pour in the cream, turn up the heat a little and simmer for a minute or so to incorporate. Season with black pepper and just a little salt – the Parmesan will add quite a bit of salt.

Meanwhile, bring a large pot of salted water to a rolling boil and add the pasta. Give it a good stir and cook until *al dente*. Drain and add to the sauce, then stir in half the Parmesan. Serve in warm bowls and pass around the remaining Parmesan.

Rabbit Lasagne

This recipe comes from *Big Flavours and Rough Edges: Recipes from the Eagle* (Headline, 2001), and was contributed by my good friend and colleague, Tom Norrington-Davies. It's hardly your conventional lasagne bolognese and, as Tom mentions in his introduction to this recipe, there is nothing authentic about game and lasagne but it is a very good thing nonetheless. The meat ragu can easily be made a day in advance and, like any stew, it just gets better after an overnight rest. I serve this lasagne simply, with a crisp green salad and some full-bodied red wine.

SERVES 6

2 rabbits, weighing about 2kg in total
4 tablespoons olive oil
2 onions, diced
4 garlic cloves, crushed
a small bunch of sage (about 30 leaves), chopped
300ml red wine
2 tablespoons tomato purée
1 teaspoon sugar
1 tablespoon unsalted butter, plus extra for greasing
350g dried lasagne (the no-precooking variety) or 250g fresh lasagne
sea salt and freshly ground black pepper

For the béchamel sauce
50g unsalted butter
50g plain flour
750ml full-fat milk
a pinch of freshly grated nutmeg
100g Parmesan cheese, freshly grated

If your butcher hasn't already prepared the rabbit for you, it is a quick and easy job. Cut off the front and back legs, following the bone structure, and chop the saddle into 2 or 3 pieces, keeping the liver and kidneys intact.

Preheat the oven to 160°C/325°F/Gas Mark 3. Pour the olive oil into a large casserole, add the rabbit pieces in one layer and gently brown them all over. Remove them from the pan and set aside. Add the onions, garlic and sage to the pan and sauté over a low heat until the onions are soft and translucent. Return the rabbit to the pan, pour in the wine, stirring to deglaze the pan, and let it bubble for a minute. Stir in the tomato purée, sugar and butter and season with sea salt and pepper. The rabbit and vegetables should be barely covered with the wine; if necessary, top up with a little water. Cover tightly, then transfer the casserole to the oven and cook for about 1½ hours, until the rabbit is tender and falling off the bone. Leave until it is cool enough to handle and then drain off all the gravy, keeping this to one side. Pick the meat off the bones and put it back into the gravy. Check the seasoning.

To make the béchamel sauce, gently melt the butter in a saucepan and stir in the flour. Cook over a low heat for 2–3 minutes, then just as it's beginning to turn nutty and golden, slowly pour in the milk, whisking all the time so it doesn't become lumpy. Bring to the boil, lower the heat and simmer, stirring occasionally, for 5 minutes. By now the sauce will be creamy and have thickened slightly. Remove it from the heat, season with sea salt, pepper and nutmeg and fold in around two-thirds of the Parmesan.

Now to put the lasagne together: generously butter a baking dish and arrange a layer of the rabbit sauce in it. Top that with a layer of pasta, then add a coating of white sauce. Start again with the remaining rabbit, then pasta and finish off with the white sauce. Sprinkle over the remaining Parmesan and leave the lasagne to sit for 30 minutes before baking.

Preheat the oven to 180°C/350°F/Gas Mark 4. Cover the lasagne with foil, place the dish on the lowest shelf of the oven and bake for 30 minutes. Remove the foil and check whether the pasta is cooked – a knife should pierce it easily – then move the dish to the top of the oven to brown the cheese. Serve straight away, while it's piping hot.

Pumpkin and Ricotta Gnocchi

Gnocchi, or little dumplings, are an Italian favourite and take pride of place on many a gastropub menu. A variation on the theme of the more popular potato gnocchi, these light and elegant pumpkin dumplings make a satisfying lunch or dinner on a cool autumn evening, accompanied by a crisp green salad.

Making gnocchi is not as complicated as it may appear. The key lies in a little organisation. Have all of the ingredients at hand and always mix the ricotta and semolina into warm pumpkin flesh; this way it will blend in quickly, giving you the soft, smooth dough necessary for the lightest of dumplings. Also, be sure to have your sauce hot and standing by before you begin poaching the gnocchi.

SERVES 4

1kg pumpkin or butternut squash
a little olive oil
300g ricotta cheese
300g fine semolina
100g Parmesan cheese, freshly grated, plus extra for serving
a pinch of freshly grated nutmeg
sea salt and freshly ground black pepper

For the tomato and sage sauce
3 tablespoons olive oil
2 garlic cloves, finely chopped
600g tomatoes, skinned and chopped
1 tablespoon finely sliced sage leaves

Preheat the oven to 180°C/350°F/Gas Mark 4. Cut the pumpkin into chunks, or cut the squash in half, and scoop out the seeds. Rub with a little olive oil, season with a pinch of sea salt and place skin-side down on a baking tray. Bake on the middle shelf of the oven for 20–30 minutes, until the chunks are soft.

Meanwhile, make the sauce. Heat the olive oil in a heavy-based saucepan and add the garlic. Stir constantly until the garlic is beginning to turn a light golden colour, then add the tomatoes and bring quickly to the boil. Turn the heat down low and simmer for 20 minutes; when the sauce is ready, the oil will separate from the tomatoes and float to the top. Stir in the sage leaves and season with sea salt and black pepper.

When the pumpkin is done, remove it from the oven, leave to cool just a little, then scrape the flesh from the skin into a wide bowl. Mix in the ricotta and semolina, beating the ingredients well to combine them thoroughly. Add the Parmesan, a small grating of nutmeg and some sea salt and black pepper. Turn the mixture out on to a board dusted with a little semolina and work it into a firm dough. If it is at all sticky, just add a little extra semolina.

Fill your largest pot with water, add a teaspoon of sea salt and bring to the boil.

Meanwhile, divide the pumpkin mixture into 4, roll each piece into a long sausage and cut it into 2cm lengths. Roll each piece over the tines of a fork; this will create distinctive ridges for the sauce to cling to. Poach the gnocchi by dropping them into the boiling water in batches. As they rise to the surface, simmer for around 2 minutes. Remove with a slotted spoon, drain and transfer to a shallow baking dish. Spoon over the tomato and sage sauce, sprinkle with some extra Parmesan and then bake in the oven at 180°C/350°F/ Gas Mark 4 for 10 minutes, until the sauce is bubbling and the cheese has browned on top.

Wild Mushroom Risotto

So often poor old vegetarians are left with very few options when it comes to eating out. I regularly hear my veggie sisters and friends moan that all they get is risotto or pasta, or horrible vegetable bakes. Veggie bakes aside, I don't see why there should be a problem with risotto. I may be an unreconstructed carnivore but out of all the European countries I think the Italians have a way with vegetables and rice, and treat them both sympathetically. I also think that wild mushroom risotto is a wonderfully intense dish and should be enjoyed by all, meat eaters and vegetarians alike.

SERVES 4

15g dried porcini mushrooms
150g unsalted butter
2 onions, finely diced
2 garlic cloves, chopped
350g Arborio or Carnaroli rice
100ml white wine
500g fresh mushrooms (a mixture of wild and cultivated), sliced
100g Parmesan cheese, freshly grated
1 tablespoon chopped parsley
1 tablespoon chopped tarragon
sea salt and freshly ground black pepper

Pour 200ml warm water over the porcini and leave to soak for 10 minutes. Drain the mushrooms, reserving the liquid, and squeeze out the excess water.

Put 1 litre of water in a pan and bring it to a simmer. In a large, heavy-based pan, melt two thirds of the butter and add the onions and garlic with a pinch of sea salt. Cover and cook over a low heat for around 5 minutes, until soft and translucent. Add the soaked porcini and cook for 2 minutes. Turn up the heat to medium and add the rice. Stir for a minute, until it is completely coated with the butter, then pour in the wine. Let it bubble, stirring constantly, until it has all been absorbed. Now add the reserved porcini liquid and around 100ml of the simmering water, again stirring constantly until all the liquid has been absorbed. Gradually add the rest of the water a ladleful at a time, still stirring, and making sure it has all been absorbed before the next addition. After 20 minutes, start checking the rice to see if it is done; the grains should still be a little bit firm to the bite. Season with sea salt and pepper, cover and leave to the side.

Melt 40g of the remaining butter in a large frying pan and sauté the fresh mushrooms with a pinch of sea salt until tender. Add them to the risotto with the remaining butter, half the Parmesan, and the herbs. Stir thoroughly until the cheese and butter have melted into the rice to form a rich, creamy mass. Serve straight away in warmed bowls, topped with the remaining Parmesan.

Cavolo Nero Risotto

Cavolo nero is an Italian variety of cabbage, its long, slender stalks not quite black, as the name suggests, but a very dark purplish green. It's much stronger and earthier in flavour than green cabbage and works beautifully in soups and in rice and pasta dishes. It is now regularly grown in the UK and can be found in farmers' markets and larger supermarkets. If you do have trouble finding it, curly kale makes a great substitute.

SERVES 4

500g cavolo nero
120g unsalted butter
2 onions, finely diced
2 garlic cloves, chopped
350g Arborio or Carnaroli rice
100ml white wine
100g Parmesan cheese, freshly grated
sea salt and freshly ground black pepper

Strip the leaves from the stems of the cavolo nero and chop them roughly. Bring 1.2 litres of water to the boil in a large pot, adding $1/2$ teaspoon of sea salt, and plunge in the leaves. After the water has come back to the boil, cook for about 5 minutes, until the leaves are soft. Drain the leaves but keep the cooking water, as this will be your stock. Pour it back into a pan and bring to a simmer. Now whiz the leaves in a food processor, adding a little of the stock, until you have a smooth purée. Set aside.

Melt two thirds of the butter in a large, heavy-based pan and add the onions and garlic with a pinch of sea salt. Cover and cook over a low heat for 5 minutes, until soft and translucent. Turn the heat up to medium and add the rice, stirring around to coat it completely with the butter. Pour in the wine and let it bubble until it has all been absorbed. Now add around 200ml of the simmering cabbage liquid, stirring constantly until it has been absorbed. Gradually add the rest of the liquid a ladleful at a time, still stirring, and making sure it has all been absorbed before the next addition. After 20 minutes, start checking the rice to see if it is done; the grains should still be a little firm to the bite.

Stir in the cavolo nero purée and season with a grind of black pepper and maybe a little sea salt – remember that the stock already has some salt in it. Add the remaining butter and half the Parmesan and stir thoroughly, letting the butter and cheese melt to coat the rice. Serve immediately in warmed bowls, topped with the Parmesan.

Shellfish Risotto

A speciality of the northern Italian region of Veneto, this risotto is bursting with sweet shellfish and uses Vialone Nano rice, grown in the nearby Po Valley. Vialone Nano has the smallest grain of the three main risotto rice varieties and has less starch on the outside, making it less creamy, and perfect for this almost soupy shellfish dish.

SERVES 6

400g clams
400g mussels
200ml white wine
120g unsalted butter
3 tablespoons olive oil
1 onion, finely chopped
1 fennel bulb, finely chopped
2 garlic cloves, finely chopped
200g cleaned squid, cut into 1cm strips
450g Vialone Nano rice
200g raw prawns, shelled
2 tablespoons chopped parsley
sea salt and freshly ground black pepper

Wash the clams and mussels under cold running water to remove any grit or sand, discarding any open ones that don't close when tapped on the work surface.

Put 1.2 litres of water in a pan and bring to a simmer. Put the clams in a separate pan with the white wine, cover and bring to the boil. The steam will open the clams in about 5 minutes. Remove the clams from the pot with a slotted spoon and set aside. Strain the liquid through a fine sieve, as it may contain a little leftover sand. Pour the liquid back into the pot and add the mussels. Cover and bring to the boil, then let the mussels steam in the same way for about 3 minutes. When all the mussels are opened, remove them from the pot. Strain the liquid into a clean pan and keep it warm on the stovetop. Pick the mussels and clams from their shells (discarding any shells that haven't opened) and set aside.

In a large, heavy-based pan, melt two thirds of the butter with the olive oil and add the onion, fennel and garlic with a pinch of sea salt. Cover and cook over a low heat for 10 minutes, until soft and translucent. Raise the heat to medium, add the squid and cook for 2 minutes. Add the rice and stir thoroughly to coat it in the butter. Pour in the shellfish cooking liquid and let it bubble, stirring constantly, until it has all been absorbed. Add around 200ml of the simmering water and again, stir constantly until it has been absorbed. Gradually add the rest of the water a ladleful at a time, still stirring, and making sure it has all been absorbed before the next addition. After 15 minutes, add the prawns, then cook for a further 5 minutes. Now check the rice to see if it is done; the grains should still be a little firm to the bite. This risotto should have a fairly fluid consistency – what Italians call *alla'onda*, or 'wavy'.

Add the clams and mussels and cook for a minute or two, until they are warmed through. Mix in the remaining butter and the parsley and season with sea salt and black pepper. Serve immediately.

Roast pumpkin

wild mushroo

Clams, white

Smoked hadd

Cod & parsley

Fish

Clams, White Beans and Chorizo
Shallow-fried Squid with Tartare Sauce
Skate, Roasties and Aioli
Cod and Parsley Sauce
Plaice, Purple Sprouting Broccoli and Anchoïade
Brill, Leeks and Red Wine
Grilled Sea Trout with Cucumber, New Potatoes, Crème Fraîche
  and Sorrel
Grey Mullet and Roast Baby Beetroot
Halibut, Peas and Lettuce
Mackerel with Gooseberries
Baked Sea Bream, Tomatoes, Olives and Parsley
Smoked Haddock Fishcakes
Wild Salmon and Cucumber
The Gun Fish Pie
Sea Bass and Salsa Romesco

Clams, White Beans and Chorizo

I wasn't quite sure where to place this recipe, as it's not really a soup, neither is it a stew or a fish dish in its own right. All I can say is that we used to sell bowl after bowl of it at the Eagle. It is the kind of dish that hits all the bases: sweet, salty clams offset by smoky paprika and tender white beans. All that's needed with it is a bib and a chunk of crusty bread to mop up the juices.

SERVES 6

250g dried white beans
3 tablespoons olive oil
4 garlic cloves, peeled
1 bay leaf
500g chorizo, cut into rounds 5mm thick
1kg clams
100ml white wine
2 tablespoons chopped parsley
sea salt and freshly ground black pepper

Put the beans in a bowl and add enough water to cover by at least 10cm. Leave to soak overnight.

The next day, drain the beans and rinse them in cold water. Put them in a pot and pour in enough fresh water to cover by 4cm. Bring to the boil, skim off any scum that forms on the surface, then add the olive oil, garlic cloves and bay leaf. Turn the heat down low and simmer for 1–1½ hours, until the beans are soft. When they are done, pick out the bay leaf, crush the garlic in the pot with the back of a spoon, then season with a good pinch of sea salt and a grind of black pepper and set them aside in their liquid.

Preheat the oven to 160°C/325°F/Gas Mark 3. Put the chorizo slices on a baking tray, place in the oven and cook for 10 minutes. They shouldn't be completely cooked but should just release the excess fat that can overpower the dish. Drain the chorizo and stir them through the beans.

To finish the dish, wash the clams under cold running water to remove any grit or sand, discarding any open ones that don't close when tapped on the work surface. Place them in a large pot with the wine, cover and bring to the boil. The steam will open them in about 5 minutes. When all the clams are open, pour them, together with their liquid, into the bean mixture and warm everything through together. Mix in the parsley and serve straight away.

Shallow-fried Squid with Tartare Sauce

For me, deep-fried squid brings to mind the chewy, battered and often previously frozen rubber rings piled into a basket with a squeezy sachet of sauce. Don't get me wrong, I do quite like these in a plasticky sort of way, but you don't get much in the way of squid flavour, as the batter tends to take over. Fresh calamari dusted with flour and quickly fried, is vastly different, and easy to cook at home without the fuss of a deep-fat fryer.

SERVES 2

500g squid
50g plain flour
sunflower oil for frying
Tartare Sauce (see page 231)
1 lemon, cut into wedges
sea salt and freshly ground black pepper

To clean the squid, hold the body in one hand and the tentacles in the other, then pull and twist – the innards and tentacles will come away together. Cut the tentacles away just underneath the ink sac and squeeze out and discard the hard beak. Pull the purple membrane off the body and remove the quill from inside the body. Cut off and keep the wings. Wash the squid thoroughly under cold running water, then drain and dry on kitchen paper. Slice the wings and tentacles into strips and then cut the body into bite-sized rings.

Put the flour in a mixing bowl and season with sea salt and black pepper. Toss the squid in the flour and shake off the excess. Heat 3cm of sunflower oil in a deep pan and fry the squid in small batches for 2 minutes, until golden – much longer and it can become tough. It's important not to overcrowd the pan or the oil temperature will lower and the squid will stew and not become crisp. Drain well on absorbent paper and serve immediately, with tartare sauce and the lemon wedges.

Skate, Roasties and Aioli

I must say that I'm a great fan of the skate wing. It has dense flesh with a sweet, delicate flavour, it comes ready prepared in a handy triangular slab and it's easy to cook. This is a fish that can take high temperatures and, dusted with a mixture of polenta and flour, will come out of the oven crisp on the outside and melting within. The combination of roasties and aioli gives it a spin on 'fish and chips', which I always prefer to get from a good chipper.

SERVES 4

1kg large, waxy potatoes, peeled and cut into wedges
sunflower oil for roasting
50g instant polenta
2 heaped teaspoons plain flour
4 skate wings, weighing about 180g each
40g unsalted butter
Aioli (see page 231)
sea salt and freshly ground black pepper

Preheat the oven to 180°C/350°F/Gas Mark 4. Put the potatoes into a large pan, cover with cold water and add a good pinch of sea salt. Bring to the boil over a medium heat and cook for 8-10 minutes, until they release their starch and are about half cooked. Drain and then dry them on kitchen paper.

Put a large baking tray in the oven for 2 minutes to get it good and hot, then pour in enough oil just to cover the bottom of the tray. Carefully add the potatoes in a single layer, sprinkle over a little sea salt and roast for 45 minutes on the top shelf of the oven, turning them at 15-minute intervals, until they are golden and crunchy.

Meanwhile, mix together the polenta and flour in a bowl and season with sea salt and pepper. Dip each skate wing into the seasoned polenta and shake off any excess. Take another baking tray, large enough to hold all 4 skate wings, and heat it in the oven for 2 minutes. Pour in enough oil just to cover the tray and then put the fish in it. Divide the butter into 4 and place a knob on top of each wing.

Place the tray in the top part of the oven, switching places with the potatoes, and bake for 8–10 minutes, depending on the thickness of the fish. To check whether the fish is done, press the thickest part of the wing; if it comes easily away from the bone, it is ready.

Divide the fish and roasties between 4 warmed plates and serve with a dollop of aioli.

Cod and Parsley Sauce

For me, cod and parsley sauce is one of those classic English dishes, and proper comfort food that rightly finds its way into pub dining rooms all over the country. It is a firm favourite at the Fox. For the sauce, I use curly parsley, now far less fashionable than its Continental cousin. I expect that's because the crinkly leaves are a bit pesky to chop, but it does have a stronger flavour, giving extra zing to the finished dish.

SERVES 4

4 pieces of cod fillet, each weighing about 180–200g
20g unsalted butter
sea salt and freshly ground black pepper

For the parsley sauce
600ml milk
1 bay leaf
a small bunch of curly parsley, finely chopped (reserve the stalks)
30g unsalted butter
2 tablespoons plain flour
a squeeze of lemon juice

First make the sauce. Pour the milk into a pan and add the bay leaf, parsley stalks and a touch of salt and pepper. Bring slowly to the boil over a low heat. Just as the milk begins to bubble, turn off the heat and leave to cool slightly, then strain the milk through a sieve to remove the stalks.

Melt the butter in a heavy-based pan and sprinkle over the flour. Cook, stirring, for 1 minute, then gradually whisk in the warm milk. Bring to a simmer, stirring all the time, then reduce the heat to the lowest possible setting and let the sauce bubble gently for 15 minutes, stirring occasionally.

Preheat the oven to 180°C/350°F/Gas Mark 4. Season the fish with sea salt and black pepper. Melt the butter in a large ovenproof dish and lay the fish in it, skin-side down. Bake until it is just cooked through; this will take about 10 minutes, depending on the thickness of the fillet.

To serve, gently reheat the sauce, if necessary, and add the chopped parsley and a squeeze of lemon juice to taste. Transfer the cod to warmed plates and pour over the parsley sauce. A big bowl of mashed potatoes would make the perfect accompaniment.

Plaice, Purple Sprouting Broccoli and Anchoïade

It's the combination here that makes this dish special. The plaice, cooked on the bone, is sweet and succulent, complemented by the slightly metallic flavour of the broccoli and the piquant kick of anchovy. Purple sprouting broccoli has grown in popularity over the last few years, so much so that growers are planting earlier to extend the short season. Usually harvested after the first frosts, it can now be found from early December through till April. There is no need to trim the slender stalks: the stem can be eaten along with the florets.

SERVES 4

40g unsalted butter
a little sunflower oil
4 small whole plaice, cleaned (heads removed, if you prefer)
800g purple sprouting broccoli
Anchoïade (see page 231)
sea salt and freshly ground black pepper

Preheat the oven to 220°C/425°F/Gas Mark 7. Take a baking tray large enough to hold all the fish comfortably, place it over a low heat and melt the butter in it. Lightly oil both sides of the fish, season with sea salt and pepper and lay them on the tray. Place on the top shelf of the oven and bake for around 8–10 minutes; they should be just firm to the touch.

Meanwhile, bring a large pot of salted water to the boil. Plunge the broccoli into the boiling water and cook for no more than 2 minutes, to retain its crunch. Drain the broccoli and then put it in a wide bowl with a good few tablespoons of Anchoïade, mixing it thoroughly to coat.

Transfer the fish to warmed plates, add a pile of dressed broccoli and serve with some boiled new potatoes on the side.

Brill, Leeks and Red Wine

Brill is an elegant but pricey fish, more often found in restaurants than your local gastropub – though when I'm offered it, I'll always find room for this fine-flavoured fish on my menu. As with other flat fish, such as plaice and sole, it is usually preferable to cook it on the bone, but for this recipe I make an exception. This is an adaptation of a dish from the Burgundy region of France, known as *en meurette*, where the fish is poached with leeks and bacon in red wine. Feel free to leave out the bacon, if you wish.

SERVES 4

800g leeks, sliced into 2cm rounds
300ml red wine
300ml fish stock or light chicken stock
50g unsalted butter
3 rashers of smoked streaky bacon, rinds removed, cut into thin strips
4 fillets of brill, each weighing about 180g
2 tablespoons chopped parsley
1 garlic clove, finely chopped
sea salt and freshly ground black pepper

Bring a pot of boiling water to the boil and plunge in the leeks. Simmer for 3 minutes or until they are *al dente*, then drain and set aside.

Pour the red wine into a pan, bring to the boil and boil rapidly to reduce by half. Add the stock and boil again for 2 minutes.

Melt the butter in a wide pan, add the bacon strips and fry gently until they are golden and crisp. Add the leeks, turning to coat them in the butter, then pour in the stock and bring to a simmer. Season the brill fillets with sea salt and black pepper and lay them on top of the leeks. Cover the pan and cook gently for 5 minutes or until the fish is done. Meanwhile, rub the chopped parsley and garlic between your fingers until they are completely combined – the French term for this mixture is *persillade*.

Carefully remove the fillets from the pan and place them on warmed plates. Stir the *persillade* into the sauce and then spoon it over the fish. Serve with steamed new potatoes.

Grilled Sea Trout with Cucumber, New Potatoes, Crème Fraîche and Sorrel

This recipe comes from the renowned Havelock Tavern in West Kensington, one of the earliest and best gastropubs in London. After a fire in 2005, the Havelock is back up and running, as excellent as ever. My thanks to head chef, Jonny Haughton, for this fine addition to the book. This is what he has to say about it:

'Wild sea trout is undoubtedly one of the culinary highlights of the summer. Although natural stocks are in decline, sea trout is now farmed organically, so it can also be obtained all year round with a reasonably clear conscience. This dish is the epitome of al fresco eating, and the warm potato salad is the perfect accompaniment for the delicately flavoured fish. If sorrel is hard to come by, consider using chopped fresh mint or dill instead. Serve with lemon wedges and a green salad.'

SERVES 4

1 cucumber
600g waxy new potatoes, well scrubbed
a small bunch of sorrel, stalks removed
4 spring onions, trimmed and very finely sliced
4 tablespoons crème fraîche
1 teaspoon red wine vinegar
a pinch of cayenne pepper
2 tablespoons extra virgin olive oil
1 teaspoon Dijon mustard
800g sea trout fillet, sliced across the grain into 4 escalopes about 1cm thick
1 tablespoon vegetable oil
1 lemon, cut into wedges
sea salt and freshly ground black pepper

Peel the cucumber, cut it in half lengthways and scoop out the seeds with a teaspoon. Then slice it into half-moon shapes about the thickness of a pound coin. Place in a small bowl and add a teaspoon of salt. Mix thoroughly and tip into a colander. Place a small plate on top of the cucumber, weight it down with a heavy object to draw out the liquid, and set aside. This step can be done several hours in advance.

Put the new potatoes in a pan of cold, heavily salted water, bring to the boil and simmer until tender. I love the Scandinavian way of cooking them with dill, if you happen to have any around. Now finely shred the sorrel and combine thoroughly in a bowl with the spring onions, crème fraîche, vinegar, cayenne, olive oil and mustard. Season with salt and black pepper.

About 5 minutes before the potatoes are done, preheat a heavy-based frying pan or ridged grill pan, leaving it on full blast to get really hot. The pan *must* be big enough to accommodate the fish with plenty of room to spare – if necessary, use 2 pans. Wipe the

fish of any excess moisture and brush it with the vegetable oil on both sides. When the potatoes are ready, drain them and leave for a few minutes, then add to the crème fraîche mixture, together with the cucumber. Mix well.

At the last minute, season the fish with salt and pepper on both sides and place skin-side down in the pan. Leave untouched for a minute or two in order to get the skin crisp. Tempting as it is, try not to peek. It is difficult to give exact cooking times because it depends on the thickness of the fish. When the edges of the fish look cooked but the centre is still raw, turn it over and remove the pan from the heat. Allow to sit in the pan for a further 30 seconds to finish the cooking. Ideally you are aiming for the centre to be slightly underdone. Serve immediately, with the warm potatoes and the lemon wedges.

Grey Mullet and Roast Baby Beetroot

Grey mullet is a tasty and inexpensive fish, caught in abundance during the summer. With its slightly earthy flavour, it is ideally suited to barbecuing or grilling. The summer months also see a wealth of baby vegetables, and the golfball-sized baby beets make an ideal partner for this robust fish. Serve with a pot of garlicky aioli on the side.

SERVES 4

1kg baby beetroot, with their leaves attached
100ml water
4 teaspoons red wine vinegar
4 tablespoons olive oil, plus a little more for the fish
4 grey mullet fillets, weighing about 220g each
Aioli (see page 231)
sea salt and freshly ground black pepper

Preheat the oven to 180°C/350°F/Gas Mark 4. Cut the leafy stems off the beetroot and soak them in cold water to revive them. Wash the beets but don't peel, or the colour will run. Place the beets in a baking dish and add the water, vinegar, oil and a good pinch of sea salt. Cover with a lid or foil and bake for 1 hour or until you can easily pierce them with a skewer. Leave until cool enough to handle, then peel or rub the skins off and return them to their cooking liquid.

Bring a pot of salted water to the boil, add the beetroot stems and boil for 2 minutes, until tender. Drain and mix with the whole beets.

Preheat a ridged grill pan or barbecue. Make a couple of slits in the skin of each fish fillet at the thicker end (this counteracts grey mullet's tendency to curl when introduced to the heat). Lightly oil the fish and season with sea salt and black pepper. Place skin-side down on the grill and cook for 2–3 minutes, until the skin is crisp. Turn the fish and continue cooking for 2 minutes, until the flesh is firm to the touch.

Transfer the fish to plates. Serve the beetroot with a spoonful of the cooking liquid and a blob of aioli.

Halibut, Peas and Lettuce

This is one of my favourite springtime dishes, making use of the first fresh peas of the year. One of the simplest and most delicious ways of cooking fresh peas is to stew them *à la française*, with bacon and shallots in a buttery stock. This slowly breaks down the sugars in the peas, bringing out their natural sweetness. The addition of lettuce at the last minute gives the dish a satisfactory crunch.

SERVES 4

100g unsalted butter
2 banana shallots, finely diced
50g smoked streaky bacon, cut into strips
500g shelled fresh peas
200ml light chicken stock
1 lettuce (escarole or iceberg), shredded
4 halibut steaks, weighing about 200g each, and preferably about 3cm thick
½ lemon
sea salt and freshly ground black pepper

Melt half the butter in a heavy-based saucepan, add the shallots and bacon with a pinch of sea salt, then cover and stew over a low heat for 10 minutes or until the shallots are soft and translucent. Stir in the peas, tossing them around in the butter to coat, and pour in the chicken stock, which should barely cover the contents of the pan. Bring to a simmer, then reduce the heat, cover and cook until the peas have just a tiny bite left to them; this could take anything from 5 to 15 minutes, depending on the size and age of the peas. You could add a pinch of sugar at this point if they are not sweet enough. Stir in the shredded lettuce, leave it to wilt, then season with a tad more salt and a good grinding of pepper.

Meanwhile, melt the remaining butter in a large frying pan over a medium heat, being careful not to let it darken or burn. Season the fish steaks with salt and a grind of pepper and lay them in the pan. Cook them for about 3 minutes on each side, until lightly coloured but not cooked right through. Squeeze over the juice from the lemon and let it bubble for a few seconds, then transfer the fish to 4 warmed plates. Pour over the buttery pan juices and serve with a spoonful of peas and lettuce on the side.

Mackerel with Gooseberries

This makes it on to the menu for only about 3 weeks of the year, due to the short gooseberry season. The best berries to use are the small, almost unripe green ones, with a sharp acidity. Old English and French recipes call for a few spoonfuls of béchamel sauce to be added to the squished berries. I find that unnecessarily fussy, preferring a dollop of plain old cream to settle the sauce down.

SERVES 4

50g unsalted butter
500g gooseberries, topped and tailed
4 large mackerel, weighing about 300g each, cleaned
100ml good thick double cream, such as Jersey cream
sea salt and freshly ground black pepper

Melt the butter in a heavy-based saucepan over a low heat, being careful not to let it colour or burn. Add the gooseberries, cover the pan with a tight-fitting lid and cook over a low heat, stirring occasionally, for about 10 minutes, until the berries collapse. Pass the berries through a fine sieve into a clean pan and set aside.

Preheat a ridged grill pan over a medium heat. Carefully slash the skin of the mackerel on both sides at 2cm intervals all the way down the fish, taking care not to cut too deeply into the flesh. Season the cavity with sea salt and black pepper and rub a little salt into the skin, too. Place the fish on the grill pan and cook for 3–4 minutes on each side, turning only once so as not to tear the delicate skin.

Add the double cream to the gooseberries and heat gently, but don't let the sauce boil. Place the mackerel on warm plates and spoon the sauce on the side. Serve with boiled new potatoes.

Baked Sea Bream, Tomatoes, Olives and Parsley

The current trend in many gastropubs, pioneered by the Anchor and Hope at Waterloo, is for sharing plates. Be it a roast rib of beef, a casserole, or duck or lamb, it seems that people like nothing more than to be presented with an outsized dish of food that they can serve up to their friends, almost like having your own party in the pub. Large fish lend themselves particularly well to this sort of presentation, with sea bass and sea bream being the perfect specimens. Either fish will do for this simple recipe.

SERVES 4

75ml extra virgin olive oil
1 sea bream, weighing about 2kg, cleaned and scaled
3 large, ripe tomatoes, cut into 2cm dice
3 garlic cloves, finely sliced
100g small black olives, pitted
100ml dry white wine
2 tablespoons chopped parsley
sea salt and freshly ground black pepper

Preheat the oven to 220°C/425°F/Gas Mark 7. Choose a gratin dish large enough to hold the fish comfortably and brush it with a little of the olive oil. Make 2 or 3 slashes through to the bone on each side of the fish, at the fleshy end close to the head. Season the fish inside and out and put it in the dish. Scatter over the tomatoes, garlic and olives, then pour over the white wine and the remaining olive oil. Place the dish on the middle shelf of the hot oven and immediately turn the heat down to 200°C/400°F/Gas Mark 6. This gentler heat will cook the fish through without drying up the liquid or singeing the fish. Bake for 30–40 minutes, until the fish is firm to the touch and the flesh is beginning to flake away from the bone. Carefully transfer the bream to a warm platter.

Tip the chopped parsley into the gratin dish and swirl it around in the cooking juices, then pour the contents of the dish over the bream. Serve immediately, with steamed potatoes.

Smoked Haddock Fishcakes

Every pub menu should have fishcakes on it from time to time. I know, however, that if I kept them constantly on my menu, that would be pretty much all I would sell, so I need to give them a break occasionally. There are numerous different types and I find myself making them from salt cod, salmon and even skate, but I also enjoy the light smokiness of a nice piece of haddock – it's perfect for this comforting national favourite.

SERVES 6

1kg floury potatoes, peeled and cut into chunks
juice of 1/2 lemon
2 tablespoons chopped parsley (keep the stalks)
1 bay leaf
1kg smoked haddock fillet
a small bunch of spring onions, finely sliced
2 organic eggs
50g plain flour
150g fresh breadcrumbs
sunflower oil for frying
sea salt and freshly ground black pepper
Mayonnaise, to serve (see page 230)
1 tablespoon dill, chopped

Cook the potatoes in plenty of boiling salted water until tender, then drain and leave them to dry in the colander for a few minutes. Smash the potatoes with a wooden spoon – they don't need to be smooth – and set aside.

Bring a large pan of water to the boil and add the lemon juice, parsley stalks, bay leaf and a touch of salt and pepper. Lay the haddock fillet in the pan and let the water slowly return to a simmer over a medium heat. Turn it right down low and lightly poach the fish for 5 minutes. Transfer the fish to a plate and leave to cool.

Put the smashed potatoes into a large bowl and add the chopped parsley and spring onions. Pull the tiny pinbones from the flesh of the fish, peel off the skin and flake the fillets directly into the bowl, keeping the chunks as large as possible. Season with a little more sea salt and a good grind of black pepper and carefully fold the fish through the mix. Divide the mixture into 12 and shape into cakes. Cover and chill for an hour.

Now you need 3 bowls. In one, lightly whisk the eggs. In the second, mix the flour with some salt and pepper. Put the breadcrumbs in the third. Dust the fishcakes with the flour, then dip them in the egg and finally in the breadcrumbs, pressing the crumbs on well so they stick.

Pour some oil into a large frying pan until it is 1cm deep and place over the heat. When it is hot, add the fishcakes (it's best to cook them in 2 batches) and fry for about 3 minutes on each side, until crisp and golden brown. Remove from the pan with a slotted spoon and drain on kitchen paper. Keep the first batch warm in a low oven while you get on with the rest.

Serve the cakes with a crisp green salad and some mayonnaise with a good tablespoon of chopped dill folded through.

Wild Salmon and Cucumber

The wild salmon is a majestic fish, strong, smooth and muscular from its upstream swim towards home. Its flavour and texture bear no relation to your run-of-the-mill, battery-farmed salmon. However, the season is a short one, running from mid June until the end of August, and, with intensive fishing and river pollution, their numbers have dwindled over the years. As you would expect, there is a price to pay for all this and for wild salmon you will pay top dollar, but even if you buy it only once or twice a year, it's absolutely worth it. Organic salmon – farmed, but in an ethical and sustainable manner – is available all year round and makes a fine substitute.

SERVES 4

1 large cucumber
2 tablespoons caster sugar
2 tablespoons white wine vinegar
30g unsalted butter
a splash of olive oil
4 wild salmon fillets, weighing about 200g each
sea salt and freshly ground black pepper

Peel the cucumber and slice it crossways as thinly as possible. Place it in a colander, sprinkle with a pinch of sea salt and leave in a sink to drain for about 30 minutes.

Put the sugar and vinegar in a small saucepan, stir over a low heat until the sugar has melted, then bring quickly to the boil. Pour the hot syrup into a bowl, mix in the cucumber and leave to pickle while you get on with cooking the salmon.

Melt the butter in a large frying pan and add the olive oil. Season the skin of the salmon with salt and pepper. When the butter begins to bubble, lay the fish in the pan, skin-side down. Cook over a medium heat for 3 minutes, until the skin begins to brown and crisp and the flesh on the sides of the fillet becomes opaque, then turn the fillets over and cook for a further 2 minutes. The salmon should be slightly underdone.

Arrange the salmon on 4 warmed plates and spoon the cucumber, along with its dressing, on the side. Serve with steamed new potatoes and pass around a pot of mayonnaise (see page 230).

The Gun Fish Pie

A fitting recipe from a fine London pub. The award-winning Gun sits on the Thames in the Docklands area of East London, overlooking Greenwich and the Millennium Dome. It's just around the corner from Billingsgate fish market, where chef Scott Wade procures the freshest fish for the Gun's signature fish pie. This is one of the few dishes that have been on the menu since day one, and I think it's fair to say there would be a riot if he ever took it off. I love the inclusion of mushy peas in the pie – clever idea.

SERVES 6–8

1kg monkfish, cut into 2cm cubes
600g salmon fillets, cut into 2cm cubes
6 leeks, trimmed
a little olive oil
2 x 400g cans of good-quality mushy peas
sea salt and freshly ground black pepper

For the court bouillon
20g unsalted butter
1 carrot, sliced
1 onion, sliced
the trimmings from the leeks (above)
1 celery stalk, sliced
$1/2$ fennel bulb, sliced
1 litre water
200ml white wine
2 tablespoons white wine vinegar
1 bay leaf
10 black peppercorns
a good pinch of sea salt

For the Mornay sauce
1 litre full-fat milk
30g unsalted butter
30g plain flour
100ml double cream
2 organic egg yolks
a good pinch of cayenne pepper
$1^{1}/_{2}$ teaspoons English mustard
100g Gruyère cheese, grated

For the mash
1.5kg floury potatoes, peeled and cut into chunks
200ml milk

First make the court bouillon. Melt the butter in a large stainless steel pan and add the vegetables. Cover the pan and leave the vegetables to soften over a low heat for 8–10 minutes. Add the water, wine, vinegar, bay, peppercorns and salt and bring to the boil. Turn the heat right down and simmer for 15 minutes.

Add the fish pieces to the pan and bring just to a simmer, then remove the pan from the heat and leave the fish to cool in the liquid.

Preheat the oven to 180°C/350°F/Gas Mark 4. Place the leeks in a baking tray, drizzle over a little olive oil and season with sea salt and black pepper. Roast for about 15 minutes, until they are soft and easily pierced with the point of a sharp knife. Leave to cool, then strip off the top 2 layers and cut the leeks into 2cm chunks.

For the Mornay sauce, warm the milk in one saucepan and then in another, melt the butter over a medium heat. Once the butter begins to bubble, quickly add the flour, stirring all the time. Cook this mixture over a low heat for 1 minute, being careful not to let it brown. Gradually pour in the warm milk, whisking continuously so it doesn't become lumpy. Simmer gently for 10 minutes, until the sauce has thickened. Add the double cream, simmer for 2 minutes, then fold through the egg yolks. Remove the pan from the heat, season with the cayenne and a pinch of sea salt, then mix in the mustard and two-thirds of the cheese.

While all this is going on, cook the potatoes in plenty of boiling salted water until tender, then drain well. Mash with the milk to make a smooth, easily spreadable topping. Preheat the oven to 200°C/400°F/Gas Mark 6.

Now to assemble the pie: spread the mushy peas over the bottom of a baking dish about 2–2.2 litres in capacity. Top them with the pieces of monkfish and salmon, then cover them with the roasted leeks. Pour over three-quarters of the Mornay sauce, shaking the dish a little so that the sauce covers everything without disturbing the layers. Cover this with the mashed potato and top that with the remaining Mornay sauce. Finally, sprinkle over the rest of the Gruyère cheese.

Bake on the middle shelf of the oven for 30 minutes, until bubbling and golden brown.

Sea Bass and Salsa Romesco

Salsa romesco is one of the great Catalan sauces and is wonderful served alongside simple roast fish, chicken, lamb or grilled vegetables. A dollop also goes beautifully into a rich fish stew. It is made by pounding roast almonds, peppers, garlic and just a touch of chilli into a heady paste, which is then loosened with extra virgin olive oil and seasoned with smoky paprika.
I like this sauce chunky, with big pieces of almond floating through it, so prefer to make it with a pestle and mortar, but a food processor will do a satisfactory job – just be sure to pulse, not whiz.

SERVES 4

4 sea bass fillets, weighing 180g each
a little olive oil, sea salt and freshly ground black pepper

For the romesco sauce
3 red peppers, halved and seeded
3 garlic cloves
1 long red chilli
125g blanched almonds
1/3 teaspoon sweet smoked paprika
2 teaspoons sherry vinegar
120ml extra virgin olive oil

Preheat the oven to 180°C/350°F/Gas Mark 4. Put the red peppers, unpeeled garlic cloves and chilli in a baking dish, rub them with a touch of olive oil and sprinkle with sea salt, then cover the dish with foil. Place in the middle of the oven and bake for 30 minutes, until the peppers are soft and have given off loads of liquid. Remove from the oven, take off the foil and leave to cool.

Meanwhile, place the almonds on a baking tray and roast on the top shelf of the oven for 10–15 minutes, until golden brown. Remove and leave to cool.

When the peppers are cool enough to handle, take them from the liquid, peel off the skin and set them aside, reserving the juice. Slip the garlic cloves from their skin, carefully peel and seed the chilli and put them with the peppers.

Pound the almonds with the peppers, garlic and chilli in a pestle and mortar until you have a thick, chunky paste. Add the paprika and vinegar, then slowly stir in the olive oil, as if you were making mayonnaise. Season with sea salt and pepper. If it seems a little too thick, let it down with some of the reserved pepper juice.

Preheat a ridged grill pan or barbecue. Make a couple of slits in the skin of each fish fillet at the thicker end to prevent it curling when introduced to the heat. Lightly oil the fish and season with sea salt and pepper. Place the fish skin-side down on the grill and cook for 2-3 minutes, until the skin is crisp. Turn the fish and continue cooking for 2 minutes, until the flesh is firm to the touch.

Transfer the fish to plates and serve a spoonful of romesco on the side.

Roast pumpkin

wild mushroo

clams, white

smoked hadd

cod & taste

Meat *Grills*

Leg of Lamb with Parsley and Olive Salad
Lamb Shoulder, Courgettes and Thyme
Pepper Steak
Steak Diane
Veal Schnitzel
Grilled Ox Tongue, Watercress and Runner Beans
The Cat & Mutton Steak and Chips
Pork and Fennel Sausages, Mash and Onions
Calf's Liver and Bacon
Calf's Kidneys and Anchovy Butter
Grilled Chicken, Fennel and Lemon Salad
Quails and Aioli

Leg of Lamb with Parsley and Olive Salad

Most pub kitchens are lucky enough to have a char grill as a standard piece of equipment, making it comparatively easy to grill larger joints of meat, legs of lamb in particular, for several people. However, you can still manage this dish at home without a professional grill. A whole butterflied leg of lamb will cook beautifully on a barbecue or a large ridged grill pan – though for the latter, a hot oven will help to finish it off. Serve the lamb with this tangy parsley and olive salad, the salty lemons giving it a touch of North Africa.

SERVES 8

2–2.5kg leg of lamb (boned and trimmed weight)
2 garlic cloves, crushed
100ml extra virgin olive oil
sea salt and freshly ground black pepper

For the parsley and olive salad
2 banana shallots, finely sliced
2 garlic cloves, finely sliced
4 plum tomatoes, seeded and cut into strips
1 tablespoon capers
100g black olives, pitted
50g preserved lemon, flesh scraped out and discarded, the rind thinly sliced
juice of 1 lemon
100ml extra virgin olive oil
roughly picked leaves from a large bunch of flat-leaf parsley

The first thing to do is butterfly the leg of lamb. Slice through the thinnest part of the boned leg, on the underside, then open it up and flatten it out. Trim off any sinew and make a few slashes through the thicker muscles – this will ensure that the meat cooks evenly.

Place the flattened-out leg on a platter. Mix together the garlic, olive oil and a few grindings of pepper to make a marinade and pour it over the lamb, massaging it in well. Cover and chill for at least 4 hours, turning the meat occasionally. Shortly before you are ready to cook the meat, take it out of the fridge and let it come back to room temperature.

Season the lamb with sea salt and another grind of pepper. Heat a barbecue or ridged grill pan to its highest temperature. Whack the meat on the grill, skin-side down, and leave it to cook until brown and crisp underneath. Turn it over and brown the other side. Turn the heat down to medium and cook for a further 30 minutes, turning it over once or twice. The heat reduction is important, otherwise the lamb will char on the outside and still be raw in the middle. If you are using a grill pan and it looks as if the meat is charring just a little too much before the half hour is up, put the pan in a hot oven (200°C/400°F/Gas Mark 6) for 5 minutes to finish the cooking. Leave the lamb to rest on a warm plate for about 20 minutes before carving.

Meanwhile, mix together the shallots, garlic, tomatoes, capers, olives and preserved lemon rind. Season with sea salt and pepper and dress with the lemon juice and oil.

To serve, toss the parsley through the salad, mixing well to coat it in the dressing. Carve thick slices of the lamb, lay them on a platter and pass around with the parsley salad.

Lamb Shoulder, Courgettes and Thyme

Shoulder of lamb isn't ordinarily the first cut of meat I'd choose for the grill, legs or chops being the pieces I'd reach for, but I make an exception for young spring lamb. Shoulder is a cut usually reserved for pot roasts or long, slow braises, as the connective tissues seize up while grilling. However, the smaller, more delicate spring lamb can be cooked quickly, and the end result is a tender and juicy joint.

SERVES 6

1.2kg shoulder of spring lamb (boned and trimmed weight)
extra virgin olive oil
100g unsalted butter
1kg courgettes, cut into 2cm chunks
2 garlic cloves, crushed
1 tablespoon thyme leaves
sea salt and freshly ground black pepper

Preheat a barbecue or ridged grill pan to a medium-high heat. Butterfly the boned shoulder by slicing through it at the thinnest point, on the underside, then flatten it out on a board. Trim off any excess fat and sinew from the inside of the meat and make a few shallow cuts in the thickest part, to ensure it cooks evenly.

Lightly oil the lamb and season it with sea salt and pepper. Slap it on the grill, skin-side down, and cook for 5–8 minutes, until the skin is brown and crisp. Turn the meat and cook for another 5–8 minutes, until evenly browned on the other side. Now reduce the heat to low and cook for 20 minutes, turning occasionally. The muscles should be firm yet springy.

Remove the lamb from the grill to a warm plate and leave to rest for 10–15 minutes before carving.

In the meantime, melt the butter in a large, heavy-based pan over a medium heat and put in the courgettes, along with the garlic and a good pinch of sea salt. Reduce the heat, cover and cook for about 20 minutes, stirring once in a while, until the courgettes have been reduced to a mush. Season with a grind of black pepper, adjust for saltiness, then stir in the thyme leaves.

Carve thin slices of the lamb, distribute between 6 warmed plates and serve with the courgettes.

Pepper Steak

Here I'm harking back to the Eighties pub bistro of suburban Sydney, where I began cooking. Alongside the ubiquitous crumbed calamari and veal schnitzels, no pub menu was complete without a steak, and Pepper Steak and Steak Diane (see page 112) were the outright favourites. The often sizeable steaks were fried in butter, smothered in a creamy, brandy-laced sauce and always served with a baked potato topped with more cream, this time of the soured variety. Hardly a meal for the cholesterol conscious. Much like in the UK, pub dining in Australia has come full circle, and you're likely to find these 'retro' mainstays on pub blackboards today, though treated with a lighter touch.

SERVES 4

40g unsalted butter
2 garlic cloves, crushed
150ml white wine
200ml chicken stock
1 tablespoon Dijon mustard
2 tablespoons canned green peppercorns
100ml crème fraîche
4 rib-eye steaks, weighing 180–200g each
a little olive oil
sea salt and freshly ground black pepper

Melt the butter in a saucepan over a low heat, add the garlic and cook for a minute or so, until soft but not coloured. Pour in the wine and stock, bring to a simmer and cook until reduced by half. Now add the mustard and green peppercorns and maybe a touch of brine from the tin – this will add extra heat. Simmer for 1 minute. Stir in the crème fraîche to finish off the sauce and leave it in a warm place while you cook the steaks.

Heat a ridged grill pan to its highest heat. Brush the steaks with a little olive oil and season them with sea salt and black pepper. Slap them on to the grill and seal well underneath before turning them over to cook the other side. How long you cook your steak depends on how you like it done. A 200g rib-eye about 2cm thick would take around 2 minutes per side for a rare steak. Leave to rest for at least 4 minutes before serving.

Put the steaks on 4 warmed plates and pour any juices from the resting tray into the sauce. Warm the sauce through and spoon it over the meat. Serve with boiled new potatoes and a crisp green salad.

Steak Diane

The original recipe for Steak Diane calls for a beaten-out or minute steak and is usually fried in much more butter than I'm using here. This is an ever so slightly healthier, updated version.

SERVES 4

40g unsalted butter
1 banana shallot, finely diced
2 garlic cloves, crushed
50ml brandy
100ml chicken stock
2 tablespoons Worcestershire sauce
1 tablespoon Dijon mustard
juice of ½ lemon
100ml crème fraîche
4 rib-eye steaks, weighing 180–200g each
a little olive oil
sea salt and freshly ground black pepper

Melt the butter in a saucepan, add the shallot and garlic and cook over a low heat for 5 minutes, until soft and translucent. Pour in the brandy, stirring to deglaze the pan, then pour in the chicken stock and leave it to simmer over a medium heat until reduced by half. Add the Worcestershire sauce, mustard and lemon juice and let the sauce bubble for a minute. Stir in the crème fraîche, season with sea salt and black pepper and leave in a warm place while you cook the steaks.

Heat a ridged grill pan to its highest heat. Brush the steaks with a little olive oil and season them with sea salt and black pepper. Slap them on to the grill and seal well underneath before turning them over to cook the other side. How long you cook your steak depends on how you like it done. A 200g rib-eye about 2cm thick would take around 2 minutes per side for a rare steak. Leave to rest for at least 4 minutes before serving.

Place the steaks on 4 warmed plates and pour any juices from the resting tray into the sauce. Warm the sauce through and spoon it over the meat. Serve with boiled new potatoes and a crisp green salad.

Veal Schnitzel

This is another firm favourite on the Sydney pub dining scene, appearing on the bistro blackboard for as long as I can remember and still going strong today. From memory, I spent an inordinate amount of time crumbing veal. It wasn't just a plain old schnitzel that was so popular but all sorts of combinations. You could have it topped with ham and melted Cheddar, or smothered in creamy mushrooms, or layered with tomato and Mozzarella. My favourite by far was 'Milanese style' – simply crumbed with a touch of Parmesan and served with a wedge of lemon. This was the schnitzel that made an easy transition from the pub to home, as a simple dinner when there was little time to cook. My mother used to make it for us once a week, and it always came with steamed new potatoes topped with soured cream.

SERVES 4

50g plain flour
2 organic eggs, lightly beaten
100g breadcrumbs, made from day-old bread
50g Parmesan cheese, finely grated
4 veal escalopes, weighing 180g each
30g unsalted butter
a splash of olive oil
lemon wedges, to serve
sea salt and freshly ground black pepper

Put the flour in a large shallow dish, the beaten eggs in another and the breadcrumbs and Parmesan in a third. Season the veal escalopes on both sides with a touch of sea salt and pepper and dust them with the flour, shaking off the excess. Dip them in the beaten egg, then toss with the combined breadcrumbs and Parmesan, pressing the crumbs lightly on to the flesh to get an even coating.

You will probably need to cook the veal in 2 batches, so preheat the oven to 150°C/300°F/ Gas Mark 2 to keep it warm. Heat the butter and olive oil in a large, heavy-based frying pan. Just as it begins to bubble, lay in 2 of the escalopes. Cook over a medium heat for 2 minutes, until the crumbs have crisped and turned a golden colour, then flip them over and cook for 2 minutes on the other side. Drain on kitchen paper and leave in a warm oven while you cook the remaining escalopes.

Put the veal on 4 warmed plates and serve with the lemon wedges and boiled new potatoes topped with soured cream.

Grilled Ox Tongue, Watercress and Runner Beans

I tend to think of ox tongue as an old-fashioned, even austere, meat. Before I started cooking it in earnest, my image of it was cheap cans of potted tongue or dried-out slices of pressed tongue on a deli counter that nobody wanted to buy. It was also a pretty scary-looking thing when raw, lolling about on the butcher's tray. But ox tongue is a beautiful and versatile meat. When poached and served warm, it has a soft, supple texture with a delicate beefy flavour. When cold, the meat is rich and smooth, with just a little bit of bite to it. In this recipe, the bars of the grill give it an extra depth of flavour.

SERVES 6

1 pickled ox tongue, weighing about 1.5kg
1 onion, peeled and halved
2 celery stalks, halved
2 carrots, peeled and halved
2 bay leaves
a sprig of thyme
10 black peppercorns
1 tablespoon Dijon mustard
juice of 1 lemon
100ml olive oil
2 banana shallots, finely sliced
600g runner beans, strings removed, sliced into 2cm lengths
3 bunches of watercress, trimmed
sea salt and freshly ground black pepper

Rinse the ox tongue under cold running water. Some cooks advocate soaking it for a few hours but I don't think that's necessary. Put it in a deep pan, cover with fresh water and bring to the boil. Ladle off any grey scum that comes to the surface, then add the vegetables, herbs and peppercorns. Turn the heat down low, cover the pot with a lid and gently simmer the tongue for 2$\frac{1}{2}$–3 hours, until is tender. The best way to test this is to pierce the thickest end with a skewer; it should go in easily, then just slip out. Remove the tongue and place on a board. While it is still warm, peel away the skin. Strain the cooking liquid into a large container, place the tongue in it and leave to cool completely; it's far easier to carve a cold tongue than a warm one.

Mix the mustard with the lemon juice, a pinch of sea salt and a grinding of black pepper, then slowly mix in the olive oil. Add the shallots and leave to stand for half an hour, until they are slightly softened. Meanwhile, bring a pot of lightly salted water to the boil, plunge in the beans and cook for 5 minutes. Drain, then refresh under cold running water.

Heat a barbecue or ridged grill pan to a medium–high heat. Take the tongue from the liquid, pat it dry with kitchen paper and slice it lengthways into slabs 1cm thick. Lightly oil the slices, then slap them on the grill and cook for 1–2 minutes, until crisp and brown

underneath. Flip them over and do the same for the other side.

To serve, add the beans and watercress to the shallots and mix thoroughly to coat with the mustardy dressing. Divide the tongue between 6 warmed plates and arrange the salad on the side.

The Cat & Mutton Steak and Chips

I count myself lucky to have one of London's best gastropubs just around the corner from my home. The Cat & Mutton in the increasingly trendy London Fields has everything a good gastropub needs: a warm, relaxed atmosphere, a welcoming smile from the staff, and great food and wine guaranteed. My regular dinner here is their superb steak and chips and I've persuaded head chef, Martin Kroon, to share his recipe:

'At the Cat & Mutton we serve our rump of beef with chips, watercress and béarnaise sauce. A really straightforward, safe dish that has never really been taken off the menu, due to customer demand. This is a dish in which the ingredients are crucial. We use the best Aberdeen Angus beef, cut along the grain and shaped into a thick tournedos; Maris Piper potatoes, twice cooked; and dressed watercress mixed with thin shallot rings. But the secret is the béarnaise sauce. We always make extra because our customers never seem to be able to get enough of it. It might sound a bit tricky but the result is well worth it.'

SERVES 4

4 rump steaks, weighing 200g each
a little olive oil
sea salt and freshly ground black pepper

For the béarnaise sauce
150g unsalted butter
50ml white wine vinegar
50ml dry white wine
1 shallot, finely chopped
3 black peppercorns
a handful of chopped tarragon (stalks reserved)
2 large organic egg yolks
a squeeze of lemon juice

For the chips
1kg Maris Piper potatoes
vegetable or sunflower oil for deep-frying

First make the sauce. Melt the butter over a low heat. Place the vinegar, wine, shallot, peppercorns and tarragon stalks in a small saucepan over a medium heat and simmer until the liquid has reduced by about three-quarters. Strain into a bowl. Put the egg yolks and the vinegar reduction into a heatproof bowl set over a pan of simmering water, making sure the water doesn't touch the base of the bowl. Using a balloon whisk, whisk until the mixture is light and frothy. The idea is to cook the egg yolk 'bubbles' slightly, but be careful not to overcook, as it can quickly turn into scrambled egg.

When the mixture is thick, take it off the heat, still whisking to cool it down slightly. Now whisk in the melted butter, a tablespoon at a time, until the sauce is thick and smooth (the butter should be at the same temperature as the egg mix to prevent it separating). Be careful not to overbeat the sauce, as it can easily separate. Stir in the chopped tarragon and season to taste with salt, black pepper and a squeeze of lemon juice. Pour the sauce into a clean glass bowl and leave it to sit in a warm place while you get on with the rest of the dish.

To make the chips, peel the potatoes and cut them into long strips 1cm thick. Rinse well under cold running water to remove the starch and then dry them on a tea towel.

Heat the oil to 130°C/260°F in a deep-fat fryer. Place a single layer of chips in the basket and lower it into the oil. Fry for about 5 minutes, until the chips are tender right through but still pale. Lift them out in the frying basket, drain off the excess oil and turn them on to kitchen paper. Repeat with the rest of the chips. At this point the blanched chips will hold nicely. You can complete the cooking when you need them.

To finish the chips, raise the oil temperature to 190°C/375°F and cook them, again in batches, for about 2 minutes, until they are golden and crisp. Drain on kitchen paper and sprinkle with sea salt and pepper.

For the steaks, heat a ridged grill pan over a high heat. Rub the steaks with a little olive oil, season one side with sea salt and a grind of black pepper, then lay that side on the hot grill. Cook for 1–2 minutes, until the steak is sealed and brown underneath, then season the uncooked side before flipping it over. Continue cooking for another minute or two. Unless your steak is seriously thick, this cooking time will deliver you a rare steak. Reduce the heat to medium and cook for another minute or so on both sides for medium rare to medium. It's crucial that you leave the steaks to rest for 5 minutes in a warm place before serving.

Pork and Fennel Sausages, Mash and Onions

What can I say about sausage and mash that hasn't been said before? Not a lot really, but it's worth reiterating the major point in such a simple dish. That is, buy the best sausages that you can find. My personal preference is for Italian sausages, and pork and fennel sausages in particular. I love their deeply savoury flavour, the crunch of the seeds and the higher than usual black pepper content, which sits extremely well with mash and syrupy braised onions.

SERVES 6

150g unsalted butter
6 large white onions, sliced
2 bay leaves
1 tablespoon balsamic vinegar
250ml chicken stock
1.5kg floury potatoes, peeled and cut into chunks
300ml milk
12–18 (depending on appetite) pork and fennel sausages
sea salt and freshly ground black pepper

Melt 50g of the butter in a heavy-based saucepan and add the onions and bay leaves with a pinch of sea salt. Cover the pan and let the onions sweat over a low heat for about 30 minutes, stirring occasionally. The onions will have released quite a bit of liquid, so now remove the lid and allow that liquid to reduce until it is a deep brown syrup. Add the vinegar and chicken stock, give it a quick bubble and season with sea salt and black pepper.

Rinse the potatoes under cold running water to remove any excess starch. Put them in a large pan, cover with plenty of cold water and add a good few pinches of sea salt, then bring to the boil over a high heat. Reduce the heat and simmer until the potatoes are tender. Drain well, return to the pan and place over a low heat so any excess moisture evaporates. In a small pan, warm the milk and the remaining butter until the butter has melted. Pour about half the milk and butter mixture on to the potatoes and mash with a potato masher or beat with a wooden spoon until the potatoes are smooth. Slowly pour in the rest of the milk mixture until you have the desired consistency, then season with sea salt and pepper.

In the meantime, preheat a ridged grill pan or overhead grill to a medium heat and cook the sausages, turning them frequently until they are golden brown and just on the point of bursting. The timing depends on the thickness of your sausages, but longer and slower is always better, as a charred raw sausage is not a lovely thing.

To serve, spoon a dollop of mashed potato on to 6 warmed plates, sit the sausages on top and pour over the onion gravy.

Calf's Liver and Bacon

One of the more readily approachable members of the offal family, calf's liver has surged in popularity in recent years. The resurrection of traditional British cooking on many top-class restaurant menus has had a trickledown effect on the gastropub, so the dishes in vogue, such as calf's liver, have become ever more fashionable.

A simply grilled piece of liver makes a delicious meal. Its subtle flavour is enhanced by the smoky bars of the grill but it does need your full attention while it's on there. The delicate flesh is easily charred and can overcook in the blink of an eye, so I suggest you cook just 2 servings at a time. Serve the liver with syrupy braised onions, mashed potatoes (see the previous recipe) and a rocket salad.

SERVES 4

40g unsalted butter
3 large onions, finely sliced
a pinch of sugar
1 tablespoon sherry vinegar
8 rashers of smoked streaky bacon
about 700g very fresh calf's liver, thinly sliced
extra virgin olive oil
1 tablespoon finely chopped rosemary
sea salt and freshly ground black pepper

Melt the butter in a heavy-based saucepan, add the onions and sugar and sauté over a medium heat for about 10 minutes, stirring occasionally. Then cover the pan with a tightly fitting lid and let the onions stew over a low heat for 30 minutes, until soft and lightly caramelised. Remove the lid, turn up the heat and pour in the sherry vinegar. Let it bubble for half a minute, then take the pan from the heat, season with a little sea salt and pepper and keep warm.

Preheat a ridged grill pan to a medium heat. Grill the bacon rashers until they are browned and crisp, then transfer them to a plate and leave in a warm place.

Wipe most of the bacon fat off the grill pan and turn the heat up high. Brush the liver slices with olive oil and evenly sprinkle over the rosemary, pressing it lightly into the flesh. Lay half of the liver slices on the pan. Cook for 2 minutes, until crisp and brown, then turn them over and cook for 1 minute more. This will give you a lovely browned outside and a juicy pink middle – the ideal slice of liver. Season with sea salt and a grinding of pepper and keep warm while you cook the next batch.

To serve, lay the liver on warmed plates, drape over the bacon slices and spoon a dollop of braised onions to the side.

Calf's Kidneys and Anchovy Butter

Opinion is divided when it comes to kidneys. Some people consider them a delicacy, while others absolutely hate them and no amount of coercion can make them change their minds. I must admit I wasn't too partial to them at the beginning of my cooking career. I appreciated their flavour but it was the texture that got to me – tough, chewy and overcooked. I was soon taught that a lightness of hand – and a good grill – was the best way to get over this culinary disaster and I have since been cooking and eating kidneys with relish.

Unlike lamb or ox kidneys, calf's kidneys have a delicate flavour and, in the French tradition, are often served with rich, creamy sauces, which I find overly fussy. This recipe, unashamedly adapted from one of Simon Hopkinson's, is my favourite way of serving them.

SERVES 4

2 veal kidneys, skinned and excess fat removed
extra virgin olive oil
sea salt and freshly ground black pepper

For the anchovy butter
50g anchovies
juice of 1/2 lemon
220g unsalted butter
1 garlic clove, crushed
1 teaspoon finely chopped rosemary

To make the anchovy butter, purée the anchovies, lemon juice, butter, garlic, rosemary and a grinding of black pepper in a food processor. Check for salt; it may need a tiny pinch. Spoon the butter on to a sheet of foil, then roll it up into a sausage shape and leave it in the fridge to chill.

Preheat a ridged grill pan. Cut the kidneys into 1cm slices and snip out the hard core. Brush with a small amount of olive oil and lightly season with sea salt and pepper. Grill over a high heat for 1 minute either side, until the meat is just sealed and juicy and pink inside – the finest way to eat a kidney. Divide the kidneys between warmed plates, slice the butter as thinly as possible and place it on top to melt over the hot kidneys. Serve at once, with a crisp green salad.

Grilled Chicken, Fennel and Lemon Salad

This is a great outdoor dish and ideally suited to a barbecue. The smoky flavour produced by grilling the chicken over real coals is more pronounced than on a conventional ridged grill pan and it does wonders in extracting an extra burst of aniseed flavour from the fennel.

For this dish, only chicken thighs will do. The darker meat is more robust and flavoursome than the breast. Be sure to keep the skin on – not only does it protect the chicken while it's cooking but, if you strip it from the flesh, it makes a delectable topping for the salad.

SERVES 4

4 fennel bulbs
2 lemons
8 free-range chicken thighs
75ml extra virgin olive oil, plus a little extra for brushing
100g green beans, such as broad beans, French or runner
100g pitted olives – green or black, use your favourite
200g rocket
sea salt and freshly ground black pepper

Cut the fennel bulbs into quarters lengthways, making sure the pieces stay intact, and put them into a stainless steel saucepan. Cover with cold water and add a good pinch of sea salt. Halve one of the lemons, squeeze in the juice from one half and drop in the empty shell. Bring to the boil, then simmer for 10 minutes, until the fennel has begun to soften. Drain in a colander and set aside.

Preheat a barbecue to a medium heat. Brush the chicken thighs with a touch of olive oil and lightly season them with sea salt and black pepper. Place them on the grill, skin-side down, cook for about 5 minutes, until the skin is golden brown and crisp, then cook for a further 5 minutes. Reduce the heat to a low flame if you have a gas barbecue – otherwise, find the coolest spot on the grill. Continue cooking for 10 minutes, until the thighs are done. The best way to check is to stick a skewer into the meat, close to the bone – the juices should run clear. Transfer the chicken to a plate and leave to rest.

Turn the grill up to a medium heat again (or locate the hot spot on the barbecue). Cut the drained fennel chunks into slices 1cm thick, brush them with a little olive oil and place on the grill. Cook for about 5 minutes on each side, until soft and slightly charred. Place in a salad bowl. Slice the remaining lemon half as thinly as you can and quickly grill the slices too, until the rind is soft. Add them to the fennel.

Meanwhile, cook the beans in boiling salted water until tender, then drain. Plunge them into cold water to cool them rapidly, so they keep their colour and crunch.

Squeeze the remaining lemon and mix the juice with the olive oil and some salt and pepper. Pour this over the warm fennel and lemon. Remove the bones from the chicken thighs, cut the meat in half and add to the bowl, along with the olives, beans and rocket. Toss around and divide between plates, or simply pile on to a platter. Serve at once.

Quails and Aioli

A great centrepiece for a casual *al fresco* lunch. What could be more tempting than a platter piled high with freshly grilled quails? There really is no polite way to polish off these meaty little birds. You need to get stuck in with both hands, prising the tender meat from the bones and dipping it in the aioli as you go.

SERVES 6

12 quails
extra virgin olive oil
4 sprigs of thyme
1 lemon
Aioli (see page 231)
sea salt and freshly ground black pepper

First prepare the quails. Using a sharp pair of scissors, cut up the back of each bird alongside the backbone right up to the neck, then cut along the other side of the backbone to remove it. Place the quail breast-side up on a board and press down on the breast with the heel of your hand to flatten the bird.

Place all the flattened birds in a large bowl and pour over a splash of extra virgin olive oil – just enough to coat. Strip the leaves from the thyme sprigs straight into the bowl and add a grinding of black pepper. Pare off a few strips of zest from the lemon, adding these to the bowl as well. Mix around and leave the birds to marinate for up to 1 hour.

Preheat a barbecue or ridged grill pan to a medium heat. Place the birds skin-side down on the grill and cook until the skin is crisp, turning at a 90-degree angle half way through the cooking to give a crisscross effect; this should take about 5 minutes. Season the underside with a sprinkling of sea salt, then turn the birds and cook for a further 5–8 minutes. To ensure that the birds are done, insert a skewer into the thickest part of the thigh; the juices should run clear. Squeeze the lemon over the sizzling birds just before you remove them from the grill to a platter. Leave the quails to rest for 5 minutes, then serve with a blob of aioli, plus a green salad and lots of crusty white bread.

Roast pumpkin

wild mushroo

Clams, white

Smoked hadd

Cod & parsley

Meat *Roasts*

Belly of Pork, Savoy Cabbage and Bacon
Loin of Pork and Quince
Pork Chops with Bubble and Squeak
Leg of Lamb, Rosemary and Garlic with Jansson's Temptation
Cold Roast Beef and Coleslaw
Duck Confit and Lentils
Duck Breast and Caponata
Venison, Sprout Tops and Chestnuts
Pigeon and Root Vegetable Mash
Partridge and Bread Sauce

Belly of Pork, Savoy Cabbage and Bacon

This is one of my favourite roasts, and very simple it is too. Taken from the underside of the pig, the belly doesn't do any actual work – unlike the leg or shoulder – so consequently has a thickish layer of fat under the skin. Many people are turned off by this extra fat but, cooked long and slow, it will gradually melt into the meat, rewarding you with a succulent, tender roast and a crisp casing of crackling. A bowl of simple braised cabbage is the ideal accompaniment.

SERVES 6–8

1.5kg boned belly of pork, skin scored at 1cm intervals
1 tablespoon fennel seeds
a little olive oil
50g unsalted butter
100g smoked streaky bacon, sliced into strips
1 onion, diced
2 carrots, diced
1 celery stalk, diced
2 garlic cloves, crushed
2 small Savoy cabbages, cored and sliced
2 bay leaves
200ml chicken stock
sea salt and freshly ground black pepper

Preheat the oven to 200°C/400°F/Gas Mark 6. Lay the pork skin-side down on a board, lightly season the flesh with sea salt and a grinding of black pepper, then evenly sprinkle over the fennel seeds. Roll the belly into a sausage shape and tie it with string at 2–3cm intervals. Generously sprinkle sea salt all over the skin and rub it in, pushing some of the salt right into the cracks. Lightly grease a roasting tray with olive oil and place the meat in it. Roast on the middle shelf of the oven for half an hour – this will give you good golden crackling – then turn the heat down to 160°C/325°F/Gas Mark 3 and continue cooking for 2–2$\frac{1}{2}$ hours. By this time the meat should be soft and tender.

Transfer the pork to a chopping board, loosely cover it with a sheet of foil and leave to rest in a warm place for 20 minutes before carving.

For the braised cabbage, melt the butter in a large, heavy-based saucepan, add the bacon and sauté over a medium heat for about 5 minutes; this should be enough time to render the bacon fat, leaving the pieces crisped around the edges. Add the onion, carrots, celery and garlic, give it a good stir and cover. Leave the vegetables to sweat over a low heat for 10–15 minutes, until they are soft and translucent. Tip in the cabbage, mixing it around thoroughly to coat, add the bay leaves, then pour in the stock. Raise the heat until the stock begins to bubble, then cover with a tight-fitting lid and turn the heat right down. Slowly braise the cabbage, stirring from time to time, and check for doneness after 20 minutes; at this stage it should still have a little bite, particularly the pieces from near the core. I prefer my cabbage quite soft, so I usually leave it to braise for a further 10 minutes. Season the cabbage with sea salt and pepper.

When you are ready to serve, take the foil blanket from the pork and snip the strings around the belly. Be careful when you take the strings off; they may have embedded themselves into the skin during cooking and, if you pull too hard, they will lift the crackling from the meat. Pour any porky juices from the board into the cabbage.

Slice the pork into thick rounds with your sharpest knife and lay it on warmed plates. Spoon on a hefty portion of braised cabbage and serve with steamed or boiled new potatoes.

Loin of Pork and Quince

The loin of pork is a majestic roast, standing tall and proud in its armour of crunchy crackling. To achieve a roast of great beauty, it is essential to buy the best piece of pork available. Always search for meat from a traditional, old-fashioned breed, such as Gloucester Old Spot or Tamworth. It will be dark and succulent and have a layer of fat under the skin, which is essential for good crackling. Score the skin with a sharp knife or razor at 1cm intervals and make sure it is completely dry before rubbing in olive oil and a good teaspoon of salt, getting it right between the cracks. Giving the roast a good blast of high heat will help to puff up the crackling before settling down to a lower temperature for gentle, even cooking, presenting you with a juicy and succulent joint.

Quinces appear in the markets from November to February. I simply braise them in butter, a little like making apple sauce. An excellent alternative to the fresh fruit is Spanish quince paste, or *membrillo*, which is easily found in delis and good supermarkets.

SERVES 6–8

1 loin of pork, weighing about 2kg, chined (i.e. partly boned but with the ribs intact –
  your butcher should do this for you)
2 tablespoons olive oil
6 quinces
1 lemon
50g unsalted butter
1 tablespoon caster sugar
sea salt and freshly ground black pepper

Preheat the oven to 220°C/425°F/Gas Mark 7. Score the pork skin at 1cm intervals. Make sure the skin is completely dry by giving it a good wipe with some kitchen paper, then drizzle the olive oil over it. Sprinkle over a good few pinches of sea salt and massage the salt and oil into the skin, getting it right between the cracks. Put the loin on a lightly oiled baking tray, skin-side up, and then on to the middle shelf of the hot oven. Roast for 20 minutes, until the skin begins to crisp and brown, then reduce the heat to 160°C/325°F/Gas Mark 3. Cook for a further 1 hour 40 minutes, or calculate the time needed, allowing 25 minutes for every 500g. To check if the pork is done, pierce between the crackling with a skewer; if the juices run clear, the roast is ready. Transfer the pork to a warmed platter, drape with a blanket of foil and leave to rest for 20 minutes before carving.

In the meantime, peel the quinces, cut away the core, then cut them into eighths, dropping them straight into a bowl of water with a small squeeze of the lemon to prevent them discolouring. Melt the butter in a heavy-based saucepan over a low heat. Drain the quince and add to the pan, along with the sugar and another squeeze of lemon juice. Cover and cook over a low heat, stirring occasionally, for 20–30 minutes, until soft. Beat the softened quince with a whisk or wooden spoon, until you have a smooth purée. Keep warm.

Cut the pork into thick slices with your sharpest knife and divide between warm plates. Add a dollop of quince purée and serve with roast potatoes.

Pork Chops with Bubble and Squeak

Bubble and squeak is traditionally pulled together from the leftovers of the Sunday roast. Potatoes, cabbage, meat and pretty much whatever is left uneaten are all mashed up together and quickly fried. The name is said to come from the noises produced by frying – the bubble of the vegetables and the squeak from the pan.

This recipe calls for it all to be freshly made and I include bacon instead of the usual leftover meat. Not too laborious a process, and well worth the effort. You can use any greens that are in season: Savoy or hispi cabbage in spring, kale or Brussels sprouts in winter, or spinach in the warmer months.

SERVES 4

1kg floury potatoes
100g unsalted butter
100ml warm milk
1 onion, finely sliced
100g smoked streaky bacon, sliced into strips
500g cabbage or greens, sliced into strips
2 tablespoons vegetable oil
4 thick pork loin chops
sea salt and freshly ground black pepper

First up is the bubble and squeak. Peel the potatoes and cut them into even-sized chunks of around 3cm. Put them into a pot and rinse under cold running water until it runs clear; this will remove the excess starch. Cook the potatoes in boiling salted water until tender. Drain well and mash with 50g of the butter and enough warm milk to make a smooth, though not too wet, mash. Meanwhile, melt the remaining butter in a heavy-based saucepan, add the onion and bacon and sauté gently for 5 minutes, until soft and translucent. Turn up the heat and fry until they have browned and are crisping up around the edges. Add the cabbage or greens, stirring to combine, then cover with a lid and leave over a low heat, stirring occasionally, until the greens are limp. Beat in the mashed potato and season with a little extra salt to taste and a grinding of black pepper. You can now either divide the bubble into patties or keep it in one large mass. Heat half the oil in a large, preferably non-stick, frying pan and cook the mixture for around 5 minutes over a medium heat until crisp and brown underneath. Carefully turn it over to achieve the same effect on the other side. Keep the bubble in a warm oven while you get on with cooking the chops.

Preheat the oven to 200°/400°F/Gas Mark 6. Heat the remaining oil in a large ovenproof frying pan. Season the chops with sea salt, rubbing a little directly on to the rind, then lay them in the pan. Fry over a medium heat for about 3 minutes on each side, until they are evenly browned and the rind is beginning to crisp. Transfer the pan to the oven and cook for 3–5 minutes, until the chops are done. Remove them from the pan and leave to rest in a warm place for 5 minutes.

Divide the bubble and squeak between 4 warmed plates, top with the pork chops and tip over any juices from resting the meat. Serve at once.

Leg of Lamb, Rosemary and Garlic with Jansson's Temptation

An organic or other good-quality leg of lamb from a decent butcher is an expensive product, increasingly bought only for a special occasion. Ordinarily in the pub I would bone out the leg, split it into muscles and cook them one at a time. It's much faster to cook smaller pieces and it's also cost effective, because you only cook as much as you need, when you need it. Each muscle is a different size, so a larger piece will feed 3 or 4 people, whereas the smaller muscles will feed just 2 at a time. However, if I were doing a roast for friends at home, I would cook the lamb on the bone, as I feel that all meat is tastier roasted this way. My absolute favourite accompaniment is Jansson's temptation, a creamy Swedish potato gratin, generously laced with anchovies.

SERVES 6

1 leg of lamb, weighing around 2kg
2 garlic cloves, thinly sliced
a stalk of rosemary, the sprigs removed in their natural clusters
2 tablespoons olive oil
sea salt and freshly ground black pepper

For the Jansson's temptation
50g unsalted butter
2 onions, sliced
2 garlic cloves, finely sliced
1.2kg large waxy potatoes, peeled and cut into slices 5mm thick
300ml milk
300ml double cream
75g anchovies in oil

Preheat the oven to 220°C/425°F/Gas Mark 7. Using the tip of a small, sharp knife, make about 10 little slits in the lamb, mostly around the thicker parts of the leg on the top and the underneath, and then press in the slices of garlic. Push the slices right down into the meat, following them with a rosemary sprig. Don't worry too much if they stick out a bit, they won't fall out during cooking and will perfume the meat beautifully. Rub the leg all over with the olive oil and season with sea salt and freshly ground black pepper.

Place the lamb in a roasting tin and pop it on to the middle shelf of the hot oven. Roast for 20 minutes, then turn the heat down to 180°C/350°F/Gas Mark 4. At this stage the leg will be nicely sealed and have a good brown crust. Cook at the lower temperature for 30 minutes for a medium rare roast, adding an extra 10 minutes if you like it medium and another 10 minutes on top of that if you prefer it well done. Transfer the lamb to a warm platter, drape over a sheet of foil and leave it to rest for at least 20 minutes before carving.

Just as you've put the lamb in the oven for its first burst of cooking, grease a large baking dish with 20g of the butter. Melt the remaining butter in a large, heavy-based saucepan, add the onions and garlic and sauté over a medium heat for around 5 minutes, until soft and translucent. Add the potatoes and stir in the milk and cream. Slowly bring the mixture to a simmer, then tip in the anchovies, along with their oil, and mix everything together so the anchovies are evenly distributed. Season with a little sea salt (remember that the anchovies are salty) and some freshly ground black pepper.

Pour the whole lot into the baking dish, cover tightly with foil and bake on the lower shelf of the oven for about an hour, until the potatoes are tender. Remove the foil, then raise the gratin to the highest shelf in the oven and cook for 10 minutes, until the potatoes are nicely browned on top.

To serve, carve the joint into thick slices, always carving against the grain, then put them back on the platter to mix with the resting juices. Spoon a hearty portion of gratin on to each warmed plate and top with slices of lamb. Pour over some of the juices and eat at once.

Cold Roast Beef and Coleslaw

As an alternative to the grand Sunday roast, this simple, unfussy lunch works brilliantly in a gastropub in the height of summer. Because the beef is served cold, it is wise to use one of the less expensive cuts. Topside or top rump benefits from slow roasting at a medium heat and a long rest afterwards will render it juicy, tender and well flavoured.

I prefer coleslaw made the old-fashioned way, with a salad cream dressing instead of the more modern mayonnaise. The vinegar and English mustard in the salad cream give the slaw a pungent kick, so there's no need for horseradish in this one.

SERVES 6–8

a little olive oil
1 piece of beef topside, weighing around 2kg
sea salt and freshly ground black pepper

For the coleslaw
6 organic eggs
50ml good white wine vinegar
2 tablespoons English mustard
200ml single cream
1 large cabbage (hispi is a good summer cabbage), very thinly sliced
2 carrots, shredded
1 red onion, finely sliced

Preheat the oven to 220°C/425°F/Gas Mark 7. Pour a touch of olive oil on to the beef and massage it into the flesh. Season with sea salt and black pepper and put it in a lightly oiled roasting tin. Place the tin on the middle shelf of the hot oven and roast for 15 minutes. This initial blast of heat will give the roast an even brown crust. Turn the heat way down to 150°C/300°F/Gas Mark 2 and continue cooking for 20 minutes for medium rare meat, adding another 10 minutes for medium. Remove the beef from the oven, transfer it to a platter and lay a sheet of foil over the top. Leave to cool at room temperature.

To make the salad cream, bring a small pan of lightly salted water to the boil and add the eggs. Simmer for 10 minutes, timed from when the eggs went in, then cool them completely under cold running water. Peel the eggs, remove the yolks (you won't need the whites) and place them in a wide salad bowl. Add the vinegar and mustard and, using a fork, mash the yolks until you have a smooth paste. Gradually stir in the cream and season with salt and pepper.

Add the cabbage, carrots and onion to the bowl and mix thoroughly to coat them in the dressing. Leave the salad to settle for half an hour or so before serving – this will help the vegetables to wilt a little and absorb the sharpness of the dressing.

To serve, slice the beef thinly, always slicing against the grain. Put it on serving plates, crumble a touch of sea salt on to each slice and spoon over some of the juices from resting the meat. Add a dollop of coleslaw and serve immediately.

Duck Confit and Lentils

Duck confit, a speciality of the southwest of France and a bistro stalwart, has made a seamless transition to gastropub standard. Duck legs preserved in this way are very versatile. They are traditionally used in hearty soups and stews but are equally good with a simple bowl of mustardy lentils or a crisp salad of dandelion, bacon and French beans.

The confit itself takes a day's preparation and it's important not to skip this. The prior salting gives the meat a deeply savoury flavour and helps to draw excess moisture from the flesh, preventing it leaking into the fat during the cooking process. Once cooked, the duck legs will keep for up to a month, covered in their fat and stored in the fridge.

Cans of duck fat are available in good delis and some large supermarkets.

SERVES 6

6 duck legs
150g coarse sea salt
2 bay leaves
2 sprigs of thyme
800g duck fat
freshly ground black pepper

For the lentils
1 onion, finely diced
2 carrots, finely diced
1 leek, finely diced
3 garlic cloves, crushed
750g Puy lentils
2 bay leaves
2 tablespoons Dijon mustard
3 tablespoons chopped parsley
a splash of extra virgin olive oil

First make the confit. Place the duck legs in a bowl and sprinkle over the sea salt and a good grinding of black pepper. Add the bay and thyme and mix around until the legs are coated in the salt. Cover and refrigerate for at least 12 hours or overnight.

Preheat the oven to 140°C/275°F/Gas Mark 1. Rinse the salt off the duck legs under cold running water, then dry them with kitchen paper. Choose an ovenproof dish in which the duck legs will fit comfortably in a single layer and melt the fat in it. Add the legs, making sure they are completely submerged in the fat, and cover with a lid or foil. Bake on the middle shelf of the oven for $1\frac{1}{2}$–2 hours, until you can easily pierce the flesh with a skewer. Remove from the oven and leave the legs to cool in the fat.

For the lentils, heat 2 tablespoons of the duck fat in a large, heavy-based saucepan and add the chopped vegetables and garlic. Cook over a medium heat, stirring from time to time, until they are just beginning to soften, then add the lentils. Cover with water, add the bay leaves and bring to the boil. Lower the heat and simmer, stirring occasionally, until the lentils are soft. This should take around half an hour. If the lentils start to dry out, just add an extra splash of water. Season the lentils with sea salt and black pepper and keep to one side while you reheat the duck legs.

Preheat the oven to 220°C/425°F/Gas Mark 7. Lift the duck legs out of the fat, scrape off any excess and place them skin-side up on a baking tray. Roast on the middle shelf of the oven for 20 minutes, until the skin is crisp and golden.

Warm the lentils and stir through the mustard and parsley with a splash of extra virgin olive oil. Ladle them on to warmed plates, top with a crisp duck leg and serve immediately.

Duck Breast and Caponata

Each of the Mediterranean countries of southern Europe boasts its own version of a vegetable stew. France has *ratatouille*, the Spanish enjoy their smoky *escalivada*, while Italy boasts *caponata*. Sicilian in origin, this dish is made during the hot summer months, when there is an abundance of tomatoes and aubergines, and is often bottled to be used as a relish during the rest of the year. *Caponata* is an eminently versatile dish, served as an antipasto or as an accompaniment to meat or fish. Its sweet and sour flavour sits perfectly alongside a rich, fatty duck breast.

SERVES 4

4 duck breasts, weighing about 200g each
a touch of olive oil
sea salt and freshly ground black pepper

For the caponata
100ml extra virgin olive oil
2 onions, chopped
3 celery stalks, chopped
2 garlic cloves, finely sliced
20g caster sugar
2 tablespoons red wine vinegar
400g ripe tomatoes, skinned and chopped
2 aubergines, cut into 2cm cubes
50g green olives, pitted
2 tablespoons capers

First make the caponata. Heat half the olive oil in a heavy-based saucepan and add the onions, celery and garlic along with a good pinch of sea salt. Cover and cook over a low heat, stirring occasionally, for 10 minutes or so, until the vegetables are soft and translucent.

Raise the heat and stir in the sugar and vinegar; this is where the sweet and sour bit comes in. Let the vinegar bubble for 1 minute, then add the tomatoes and simmer gently for 20 minutes, stirring occasionally, until the sauce has thickened.

While all this is going on, heat the remaining oil in a large frying pan. Lightly salt the aubergine cubes and sauté them, in batches if necessary, over a high heat. They will absorb the oil fairly quickly, so if you think you need more, add a little by trickling it down the sides of the pan so as not to lower the heat and let the aubergines stew. Reduce the temperature and continue to cook over a medium heat until the aubergines are browned and tender. Tip them into the tomato sauce and add the olives and capers. Simmer for 5 minutes, then check the seasoning.

Preheat the oven to 200°C/400°F/Gas Mark 6. Score the skin of the duck breasts, cutting only through to the fat, not the flesh, and making diagonal incisions to form diamond shapes. Rub with a little olive oil and sprinkle on some sea salt, rubbing it into the skin well. Wipe a large cast iron pan with a smear of olive oil and place it over a high heat. When the pan is good and hot, lay the duck breasts in it, skin-side down, then lower the heat to medium. Cook for 5 minutes, until the skin is crisp and brown. Pour off any excess fat, turn the breasts over on to the fleshy side, then place the pan in the oven and cook for 8–9 minutes. Transfer the duck breasts to a warm plate and leave to rest for 5 minutes.

To serve, slice the duck breasts neatly and arrange them on warmed plates, with a spoonful of caponata at the side.

Venison, Sprout Tops and Chestnuts

Sprout tops, like all hardy winter greens, begin to emerge after the first frosts, and even though they are the bushy ends of the plant they don't have a strong sprout flavour; their taste is closer to that of a hispi or Savoy cabbage. These humble greens have become ridiculously trendy in the last couple of years, finding their way out of farmers' markets and not only on to gastropub menus but right up there with the truffles and foie gras of the Michelin tribe. Chestnuts are a popular embellishment for sprout tops and for this dish you could roast and shell your own. That's quite a tedious job, though, so I suggest getting vacuum-packed ones from a deli or good supermarket instead.

Here the venison is roasted as you would a leg of lamb.

SERVES 6

1 leg of venison, weighing about 2kg on the bone
2 tablespoons olive oil
30g unsalted butter
100g smoked streaky bacon, diced
2 small onions, diced
2 carrots, diced
2 celery stalks, diced
3 garlic cloves, crushed
1kg Brussels tops, stripped from the stalks
200ml light chicken stock
250g packet of peeled chestnuts, roughly chopped
sea salt and freshly ground black pepper

Preheat the oven to 220°C/425°F/Gas Mark 7. Place the venison leg in a roasting tin, pour over the olive oil and massage it into the flesh. Season the meat liberally with sea salt and black pepper and place it in the centre of the hot oven. Roast on this high heat for 20 minutes, by which time the venison will be sealed and already have a proper roasted crust. Turn the heat down to 160°C/325°F/Gas Mark 3 and continue cooking for 30 minutes for a medium rare roast, 40 minutes for medium or 50 minutes for well done. Remove the venison from the oven, place it on a warmed platter and cover loosely with a blanket of foil. Leave in a warm place to rest for at least 20 minutes before carving.

In the meantime, melt the butter in a heavy-based saucepan, add the bacon and fry gently, stirring it around until some of the fat has rendered and it is becoming crisp around the edges. Add the onions, carrots, celery and garlic, stir around to coat the vegetables in the bacon fat, then cover the pan and turn the heat down low. Cook for 10 minutes, stirring occasionally, until the vegetables are soft and translucent. Add the Brussels tops and stock and bring to the boil. Season with sea salt and pepper, cover the pan and cook over a medium heat for 20 minutes, until the tops are only just beginning to soften; it's nice to have a little bite left. When you are ready to serve, stir in the chestnuts and simmer for a minute or so to warm them through.

To serve, carve the joint into thick slices, always carving against the grain, then put them back on the platter to mix with the juices from resting the meat. Spoon generous portions of sprout tops on to warmed plates, top with slices of venison and pour over the juices.

Pigeon and Root Vegetable Mash

Pigeons may not be the most sophisticated of the game birds but they are tasty, inexpensive and available all year round. These meaty little creatures look slightly top heavy, their breast a tad large for their size. They boast a light gamy flavour and dark red flesh, and only need a quick roast in a hot oven to cook them to perfection.

The most common variety found in shops is the wood pigeon, though even supermarkets only seem to stock them throughout the game season from September to March. However, the farmed squab pigeon, mostly reared in France, can be regularly found in good butcher's shops.

SERVES 6

60g unsalted butter
a splash of olive oil
6 pigeons, either wood pigeons or squabs
1 tablespoon rosemary leaves
3 garlic cloves, sliced in half
sea salt and freshly ground black pepper

For the root vegetable mash
1 celeriac
a squeeze of lemon juice
2 large, waxy potatoes
1 swede
2 large carrots
3 garlic cloves, peeled
100ml full-fat milk
150g unsalted butter

The first thing to do here is to prepare the mash. Peel the celeriac and cut it into 2cm chunks, dropping them into a pot of cold water with a squeeze of lemon juice to prevent discolouration. Peel the potatoes and swede and chop them into chunks twice the size of the celeriac, as they cook much faster. Peel the carrots and slice them into 1cm rounds. Add them to the pot along with the potatoes, swede and garlic. Thoroughly rinse all the vegetables, then cover with plenty of fresh water, add a teaspoon of sea salt and bring to the boil. Reduce the heat to medium and simmer for 15 minutes or so, until the vegetables are tender. Drain really well, return them to the pot and dry off any excess moisture over the lowest possible heat. Warm the milk and butter together in a small pan until the butter has melted, then pour it into the pot and crush the vegetables with a potato masher. Beat the mash with a whisk or a wooden spoon until smooth, then season with black pepper and maybe a touch more sea salt.

Preheat the oven to 190°C/375°F/Gas Mark 5. Melt 20g of the butter with the olive oil in a large ovenproof frying pan. Season the pigeon cavities with sea salt and black pepper. Divide up the remaining butter and push it into the cavities with the rosemary and garlic. Gently brown the birds all over in the melted butter, then sit them upright and place the pan on the middle shelf of the hot oven. Roast for 9–10 minutes; by then the breast meat

should feel quite tight and the butter inside the birds should be just melted. Transfer the pigeons to a warmed plate, pour over the melted butter and leave them to rest, breast-down, for 10 minutes.

To serve, spoon a dollop of the vegetable mash on to warmed plates, place the pigeons on top, then pour the resting juices over the birds.

Partridge and Bread Sauce

For me, partridge is synonymous with Christmas, and this is the bird I would choose to put on my menu in the run-up to the festive season. I can never rustle up much enthusiasm for turkey and all the trimmings. I'll happily devour it on the big day, but it's certainly not an appropriate dish for a pub menu. I also think that at Christmas people like to be offered something a bit special, and partridge absolutely fits the bill. The most highly prized partridge is the grey leg – always my first choice. These birds are native to Britain and possess the richest, gamiest flavour. The more common variety is the farmed red leg, an interloper from France that is extensively reared and not nearly as tasty as our home-grown birds. I like to serve partridge with lots and lots of bread sauce and buttered Brussels sprouts.

SERVES 6

80g unsalted butter
6 partridges
sea salt and freshly ground black pepper

For the bread sauce
500ml full-fat milk
80g unsalted butter
10 cloves
1 small onion, peeled and finely diced
1 bay leaf
a sprig of thyme
50ml double cream
120g fresh white breadcrumbs

Start with the bread sauce. Heat the milk in a pan with the butter, cloves, onion, bay and thyme and let it simmer gently for 10 minutes, making sure it never comes to the boil. Remove from the heat and leave to infuse. This can all be done a few hours in advance, if you wish.

Preheat the oven to 190°C/375°F/Gas Mark 5. To cook the partridge, melt 20g of the butter in a large, ovenproof frying pan. Season the insides of the birds with sea salt and black pepper, then divide up the remaining butter and pop it into each cavity. Gently brown the birds all over in the butter, then sit them upright. Place the pan on the middle shelf of the oven and roast the birds for 10–12 minutes, until the breast meat feels firm but just a little springy. Transfer the birds to a warmed plate, pour any melted butter from the pan over them and leave to rest, breast down, for 10 minutes.

Meanwhile, strain the milk for the bread sauce into a clean pan. Add the double cream and reheat gently, then whisk in the breadcrumbs. Let the sauce thicken over a low heat – this will only take a minute – then season with sea salt and plenty of black pepper.

Put each bird on a warmed plate along with a generous spoonful of bread sauce and pour the buttery resting juices over. Serve immediately.

Roast pumpkin

wild mushroo

Clams, white

Smoked hadd

Cod & parsley

Meat *Braises*

Shoulder of Lamb with Butterbeans and Aioli
Overnight Shoulder of Mutton
Pot Roast Brisket
Rabbit and Mustard
Gammon and Caper Sauce
Lamb's Sweetbreads, Peas and Tarragon
Duck, Prunes and Saffron
Braised Oxtail

Shoulder of Lamb with Butterbeans and Aioli

A long, slow braise is the best method for cooking the tougher, less expensive cuts of lamb, such as the shoulder. The one drawback of the shoulder is that it can be rather fatty, especially in an older animal, so ask your butcher to trim off any excess fat – and while you're there, get them to tie the joint for you too, the shoulder being quite misshapen and a bit tricky to tether. I add the pre-soaked beans to cook alongside the lamb so they absorb all the sweet flavours of the meat, garlic and herbs.

SERVES 6

300g butterbeans
4 tablespoons olive oil
1 boned and rolled shoulder of lamb, weighing 1.5–2kg
2 onions, diced
200ml white wine
1 head of garlic, divided into cloves and peeled
2 stalks of rosemary
2 bay leaves
water or light chicken stock to cover
Aioli (see page 231)
sea salt and freshly ground black pepper

Put the beans in a large bowl and add enough water to cover by at least 10cm. Leave to soak overnight and then drain.

Preheat the oven to 140°C/275°F/Gas Mark 1. Heat 3 tablespoons of the olive oil in a large, cast iron casserole. Season the lamb with sea salt, add to the casserole and brown all over on a medium to low heat. Transfer the lamb to a plate, then add the remaining oil to the pan and sauté the onions over a low heat for 5 minutes, until soft and translucent. Return the lamb to the pan with the onions, pour over the wine and let it bubble for a minute. Now add the butterbeans, garlic, rosemary and bay with enough water or light chicken stock just to cover. Bring it all to a simmer and season with black pepper and just a little more sea salt. Cover the casserole with a close-fitting lid or some foil and place it on the middle shelf of the oven. Cook for 2–2½ hours, until the meat is meltingly tender and the beans are soft and plump.

Remove the rosemary stalks and bay leaves from the dish. Carve the lamb into chunks and serve in warmed bowls with the beans and a blob of aioli.

Overnight Shoulder of Mutton

Just like music and fashion, food is susceptible to trends, and right now mutton is having its moment. Of the many mutton dishes that are gracing pub menus, the slow-braised shoulder from the King William in Bath is one of the best. Here is Charlie Digney's recipe. He comments:

'If your oven isn't large enough to accommodate a whole shoulder of mutton, you could cut it into portions with a bone saw (your butcher will do this if you ask him nicely) and braise them in a casserole instead. Or buy half a shoulder to serve 6 – the cooking time will be about the same.'

I have not given quantities for the green sauce, as it is a forgiving recipe and you can alter the proportions depending on what it is for. Add more tarragon for fish, mint for lamb or mutton.

SERVES 12

2 tablespoons goose fat or olive oil
1 shoulder of mutton, weighing about 4.5kg
1 leek, finely diced
2 carrots, finely diced
2 celery stalks, finely diced
1 head of garlic, divided into cloves and peeled
24 shallots, peeled
a handful of dried apricots
½ bottle of red wine
500ml decent mutton or lamb stock
6 sprigs of thyme
2 sprigs of rosemary
sea salt and freshly ground black pepper

For the green sauce
a large bunch of flat-leaf parsley
mint
tarragon
chervil
sage
thyme
a handful of capers
½ head of garlic, divided into cloves and peeled
1 tablespoon English mustard
6 anchovy fillets
olive oil

Preheat the oven to 110°C/225°F/Gas Mark ¼. Heat the goose fat or olive oil in a large pan, add the mutton and brown it all over. Transfer the meat to a large roasting tin, add the vegetables and dried apricots, then pour in the wine and stock. Strip the stalks from the herbs and add the leaves to the tin. Season the meat with salt and pepper and then cover the tin with foil. Put it in the bottom of your oven and leave overnight or for 12 hours. The mutton should be soft and yielding, but not falling apart.

To make the green sauce, whiz all the ingredients in a blender or food processor, adding enough olive oil to make a smooth paste.

When the mutton is done, transfer it to a platter and keep warm. Strain off the cooking juices from the vegetables into a clean pan and skim off the fat that rises to the top. Bring to the boil and simmer until reduced by half. Taste and adjust the seasoning if necessary, then return this gravy to the vegetables.

Slice the mutton thickly and serve with the gravy, vegetables, green sauce and some mashed potatoes.

Pot Roast Brisket

A pot roast of brisket is a thrifty way of doing a roast for a large number of people. An inexpensive cut, the brisket itself is a lean piece of meat from the undercarriage of the cow, covered with a thin layer of fat that helps to keep it moist and tender through the long, slow cooking process. After only a small amount of preparation, the brisket can be left to look after itself, rewarding you with a soft and unctuous texture and ready-made gravy.

SERVES 8–10

2–3 tablespoons vegetable oil
1 rolled brisket of beef, weighing around 2kg
10 banana shallots, peeled
10 small carrots, peeled
10 garlic cloves, peeled
300ml red wine
3 bay leaves
2 sprigs of thyme
500ml water or light chicken stock
sea salt and freshly ground black pepper

Preheat the oven to 120°C/250°F/Gas Mark $^1/_2$. Choose a casserole dish that will hold the beef and vegetables snugly. Heat the vegetable oil in the casserole, season the brisket with sea salt and then add it to the pan. Gently brown the meat over a low heat, turning it from time to time to seal evenly. Transfer to a plate.

Add the shallots, carrots and garlic to the casserole and sauté for 2 minutes, then pour in the wine, letting it bubble for 1 minute. Place the beef back in the pan, arranging the vegetables around it, and tuck in the herbs. Pour in the water or stock, bring to a simmer and season with pepper and a touch more salt. Cover the casserole with a tight-fitting lid and transfer to the middle shelf of the oven. Cook for $2^1/_2$–3 hours, until the meat is soft and giving, surrounded by rich gravy. Serve slices of beef in deep bowls, swimming in gravy, with the vegetables and some mashed potato.

Rabbit and Mustard

A soothing, creamy braise, this dish is the perfect way to introduce the concept of bunny eating to the scared and uninitiated. I've never had a problem with eating rabbit, even as a child, and don't really understand some people's trepidation about eating our furry friends when they have no qualms about tucking into a plate of lamb or devouring little chickens.

Wild rabbit meat is delicious, with a slightly gamy flavour. It is lean and delicate, however, and needs careful cooking to prevent it becoming dry and tough. To that end, the addition of bacon helps lubricate the dish and give it an extra savoury kick. Tame rabbits are more readily available. They are not as tasty, though, being bred mostly for their size and their white flesh. Reared in pens, they are really no better than battery chickens.

SERVES 6–8

2 wild rabbits, weighing around 2kg in total
50g unsalted butter
a touch of olive oil
1 onion, diced
2 celery stalks, diced
1 leek, diced
2 garlic cloves, crushed
150g smoked streaky bacon, sliced into strips
200ml white wine
400ml light chicken stock
1 bay leaf
a sprig of thyme
200ml double cream
3 tablespoons Dijon mustard
sea salt and freshly ground black pepper

First you need to joint the rabbits. Following the bone structure, cut off the front and back legs, then chop the saddle into 2 or 3 pieces.

Preheat the oven to 160°C/325°F/Gas Mark 3. Melt the butter and olive oil in a large, cast iron casserole, lightly season the rabbit pieces with sea salt, then add them to the pan. Gently brown the pieces over a medium heat, taking care not to burn the delicate meat or let the butter darken. Remove them from the pan and set aside. Add the onion, celery, leek, garlic and bacon to the pan and sauté over a low heat for 8–10 minutes, until the vegetables have softened.

Return the rabbit pieces to the casserole and pour in the wine, letting it bubble for a minute. Pour in the stock, bring to the boil and season with a little more sea salt and a grinding of black pepper, then tuck in the herbs. The rabbit and vegetables should be barely covered with the stock – if necessary, top it up with a little water. Cover the casserole with a tightly fitting lid or foil and place on the middle shelf of the oven. Cook for about 1¼ hours, until the rabbit is tender and falling off the bone.

Take the casserole from the oven and transfer the rabbit pieces to a warm plate. Place the casserole back on the stovetop over a high heat and pour in the cream, letting it bubble until the sauce has thickened slightly. Stir in the mustard, then return the rabbit pieces to the pan to warm through again. Don't let them cook too much or you risk them toughening and will lose the kick of the mustard. Serve with a big bowl of mashed potato.

Gammon and Caper Sauce

Gammon has been a standard on pub menus since time immemorial, though usually in the guise of a gammon steak with pineapple, smothered in an overly sweet sauce or topped with a fried egg and surrounded by chips. Poached gammon is a completely different animal and, as one of the great British classics, has returned triumphantly to become part of the gastropub repertoire. The caper sauce is very English, just a little old fashioned and a sharp foil to the gentle flavour of the poached meat.

This is a great joint for feeding a hungry crowd, and with any luck there will be enough leftovers for a round of sandwiches.

SERVES 6–8

1 smoked gammon joint on the bone, weighing 2–2.5kg
1 onion, peeled and halved
1 leek, trimmed and halved lengthways
10 black peppercorns
a couple of sprigs of thyme
2 bay leaves
100ml white wine vinegar
6 carrots, peeled and halved lengthways
70g unsalted butter
40g plain flour
2 tablespoons capers in brine, squeezed and chopped
2 tablespoons chopped parsley
sea salt and freshly ground black pepper

Soak the gammon overnight in cold water; this will leach out any excess salt.

The next day, choose your largest pot, big enough to hold the whole gammon, and place the joint in it, along with the onion, leek, peppercorns, thyme and bay. Cover the meat with fresh water, pour in the vinegar and bring to the boil over a high heat. Turn the heat down low, cover the pot and leave it to simmer for around 2 hours – to determine the exact cooking time, allow 30 minutes for every 500g. After about 1$^1/_2$ hours, add the carrots to the pot – they will then be al dente when you serve the gammon.

When the meat is done, leave it to rest in the cooking liquor for at least 20 minutes while you make the caper sauce. First, strain off 1.2 litres of the gammon stock – there should still be plenty left over to cover the joint (and to make into a soup the next day). Melt the butter in a heavy-based saucepan and, just as it starts to bubble, quickly whisk in the flour. Cook this mixture over a low heat for about 2 minutes, until it is just beginning to colour and gives off a nutty aroma. Take the pan off the heat and gradually pour in the gammon stock, whisking constantly. Return the pan to the heat and slowly bring the sauce to a simmer, stirring from time to time. Cook gently until it has thickened to the consistency of double cream. Keep warm while you carve the gammon.

Remove the gammon from the pot. A good trick is to lift it out while wearing a clean pair of rubber gloves – this way you can get a firm grip on the joint without risking dropping it and scalding yourself. Peel the skin from the leg, carve the gammon into thick slices and

place on a large platter, or divide between serving plates. Just before serving, stir the capers and parsley into the white sauce, season with a grinding of pepper and maybe a little salt, then pour it into a warm jug. Pass the sauce around alongside the gammon, together with the carrots and some new potatoes.

Lamb's Sweetbreads, Peas and Tarragon

As partial as I am to all offal, I must say that sweetbreads, particularly lamb, are my favourite offally treat. They may scare some people, as you just can't get away from the fact that they are glands, to put it bluntly. But they taste creamy and delicate, with a distinctly lamby flavour.

Taken from around the heart muscle or throat of young sheep, sweetbreads are at their best and plumpest in the spring. After that, as the sheep grow, the glands shrink away to become smaller, tougher morsels. They are far more popular on the Continent than they are here, where you will almost certainly need to order them in advance from your butcher – though if you are lucky enough to have a Turkish food store nearby, their meat counters will most likely include them.

SERVES 4

800g lamb's sweetbreads
1 tablespoon white wine vinegar
2 bay leaves
60g unsalted butter
2 teaspoons sherry vinegar
400ml lamb or chicken stock
500g shelled fresh peas
100ml double cream
leaves from 2 sprigs of tarragon, chopped
sea salt and freshly ground black pepper

To prepare the sweetbreads, soak them for around 3 hours in several changes of cold water – this is to extract any remaining blood, so the water needs to run clear. Drain the sweetbreads and place them in a saucepan. Cover with cold water and add the vinegar, bay leaves, a pinch or two of sea salt and a grinding of pepper. Slowly bring to a simmer over a medium heat but do not let the water boil or the delicate breads will toughen. Simmer for 1 minute, then drain and refresh under cold running water. Peel away the solidified fat and membrane, then lay the sweetbreads on a tea towel to dry.

Melt 40g of the butter in a large sauté pan and fry the sweetbreads over a high heat for about 2 minutes on each side, until they are golden and crisp. Add the sherry vinegar, stirring to deglaze the pan, then add the stock and peas. Simmer for about 5 minutes, until the peas are cooked. To finish the dish, pour in the cream, let it bubble, then swirl in the remaining butter and season to taste. Sprinkle in the chopped tarragon and ladle into deep warmed bowls.

Serve with steamed Jersey Royal potatoes.

Duck, Prunes and Saffron

Not quite your conventional duck stew, this is a little bit French, a little bit Spanish but completely Moorish in flavour. The French bit comes from braising the duck legs with prunes. They have a natural affinity and are cooked together throughout southern France – particularly round Agen, where the finest prunes are found. The Spanish bit is the addition of saffron, which comes from the Moorish-influenced south of Spain. There is no real tradition of combining these three ingredients, though with one degree of separation, substituting raisins for prunes, the dish takes on a very Spanish style.

SERVES 6

1 tablespoon vegetable oil or other neutral oil
6 duck legs
12 shallots or small onions, peeled
4 garlic cloves, sliced
100ml white wine
30 Agen prunes, pitted
400ml light chicken stock
a good pinch of saffron stamens
2 bay leaves
sea salt and freshly ground black pepper

Preheat the oven to 160°C/325°F/Gas Mark 3. Heat the oil in a cast iron casserole or baking dish that will hold the duck legs in a single layer. Lightly season the duck legs with sea salt and place them skin-side down in the dish. Fry over a low heat for 6–7 minutes, moving them around so they all catch the heat, until the skin is crisp and brown. Pour the excess fat from the dish (you can keep this for roasting potatoes later), then add the shallots. Cook them over the lowest possible heat until they are evenly browned. Add the garlic and sauté gently for 1 minute, then reintroduce the duck legs, arranging them, this time skin-side up, in a single layer or overlapping slightly. Pour in the white wine and let it bubble for a few minutes. Add the prunes, stock, saffron and bay leaves and bring to a simmer. Season with a grinding of pepper and check the sauce for salt. Cover the dish with a tight-fitting lid or foil and place on the middle shelf of the oven. Bake for $1^1/_4$–$1^1/_2$ hours, until the meat is tender and almost falling off the bone and the prunes are plump and juicy.

Remove the legs from the cooking liquor and keep them warm while you remove excess oil from the sauce. To do this, place the casserole over a low heat, slowly bring the sauce to a simmer and skim off the fat from the top. Pop the legs back in to heat them through. Season with salt and pepper and serve immediately, with a grain such as couscous or soft polenta.

Braised Oxtail

This delectably sticky stew is a perennial gastropub favourite. The gelatine-rich bones of the tail make for an intense and viscous braise and, after long, slow cooking, the meat will arrive on the plate wonderfully tender and melting, soft enough to cut with a spoon. Pass around bibs and fingerbowls when you serve up this stew. Half the fun of eating oxtail is gnawing and sucking at the bones – a very messy business indeed.

SERVES 6–8

3 tablespoons plain flour, seasoned with salt and pepper
1.5kg oxtail, trimmed of excess fat
2 tablespoons vegetable oil
2 onions, chopped
2 carrots, chopped
2 celery stalks, chopped
3 garlic cloves, sliced
300ml red wine
1.5 litres beef stock or water
2 bay leaves
a couple of sprigs of thyme
3 or 4 strips of orange zest, white pith removed
sea salt and freshly ground black pepper

Preheat the oven to 140°C/275°F/Gas Mark 1. Put the seasoned flour in a plastic bag and add the oxtail. Shake the bag until all the pieces are evenly coated. Heat the oil in a cast iron casserole and gently brown the oxtail in it, being very careful not to singe the flour. Transfer to a plate with a slotted spoon. Add the onions, carrots, celery and garlic to the pan with a small pinch of sea salt and sauté for 5 minutes, adding a touch more oil if you need to, until the vegetables are just beginning to soften. Tip the oxtail back into the pan and deglaze with the red wine, scraping the bottom and sides of the pan with a wooden spoon to dislodge any crusty lumps of goodness. Add the stock or water, along with the herbs and orange zest, and slowly bring to a simmer. Check the seasoning – you may need just a touch more – cover the pot tightly with a lid or foil and place it on the middle shelf of the oven. Oxtail needs a long, slow braise, as the meat can be fairly tough, so depending on the size of the joints start checking after $2^{1}/_{2}$ hours to see if the meat is tender and falling off the bone. It can take anything up to $3^{1}/_{2}$ hours.

When the tails are done, strain the sauce into a clean pan, bring it back to the boil and skim the fat from the surface. If it is a little thin, simmer it until it thickens, then pour it back over the meat. If you are serving this stew on the same day, try to leave it to cool completely first. This is just the same as resting a roast, and the meat will relax and absorb more of the sauce.

To serve the stew, gently bring it to a simmer, make sure it's piping hot, then ladle it into deep bowls. Accompany with buttery mashed potato or soft polenta.

Roast pumpkin

wild mushroo

Clams, white

Smoked hadd

Cod & parsley

Bar Meals

Cottage Pie
Pork, Cider and Potato Pie
Chicken and Leek Pie
Gypsy Eggs (Huevos a la Flamenca)
Lancashire Hot Pot
Kedgeree
Neck of Lamb and Barley
Sausage and Bean Casserole
Ham and Chicory Gratin
Macaroni, Porcini and Parmesan Cheese
Faggots and Mash
Steak and Kidney Pudding

Cottage Pie

For a long while I believed that cottage pie was called Kosciusko pie, after the highest mountain in Australia. I have since learned that this was a name used by my mother as a cunning plan to get the children (all six of us) to eat it. It worked, and this recipe comes courtesy of her cookbook. The name 'cottage pie' works fine on the bar at the Fox, though.

SERVES 4

2 tablespoons vegetable oil
1 large onion, diced
2 carrots, diced
1 leek, diced
1 celery stalk, diced
1kg minced beef
1 tablespoon tomato purée
150ml light stock or water
1 bay leaf
1 tablespoon Worcestershire sauce
sea salt and freshly ground black pepper

For the topping
1kg floury potatoes, such as King Edward or Maris Piper, peeled and cut into chunks
100ml full-fat milk
60g unsalted butter

Heat the oil in a large, heavy-based saucepan, add the onion, carrots, leek and celery with a pinch of sea salt and sauté over a low heat for 10 minutes or so, until they are soft and translucent. Increase the heat to medium and throw in the minced beef. Fry until it is sealed and browned, stirring and turning it over to break up any clumps. Add the tomato purée, stock or water, bay leaf, Worcestershire sauce and some seasoning and bring to a simmer. Cover the pan and leave it to bubble away gently while you get on with the potato topping.

Preheat the oven to 200°C/400°F/Gas Mark 6. Cook the potatoes in plenty of boiling salted water until tender, then drain well. Warm the milk and butter together in a small pan until the butter has melted, pour it into the potatoes and beat with a whisk or wooden spoon until smooth and easily spreadable. Season to taste.

Pour the mince into a casserole or baking dish and cover with the mashed potatoes, which you can fashion into mountain peaks. Dot the top with a little extra butter if you like, then bake for 30 minutes, until bubbling hot and golden brown.

Pork, Cider and Potato Pie

Pork neck is one of the more thrifty cuts, and not one that you would come across on the supermarket meat aisle. A great shame, since it has all the qualities I look for in a braising cut – not much fat or sinew but just enough connective tissue to break down into soft pillows of succulent meat. I think of this recipe as a kind of West Country hot pot, the perfect dish to tuck into on a breezy autumn day, fork in one hand, and pint of cider in the other.

SERVES 6

2 tablespoons olive oil
1.5kg pork neck, diced
1 large onion, diced
2 carrots, diced
1 leek, diced
2 garlic cloves, crushed
1 tablespoon plain flour
300ml dry cider
300ml light chicken stock or water
1 bay leaf
a sprig of thyme
1kg waxy potatoes, peeled and thinly sliced
30g unsalted butter, melted
sea salt and freshly ground black pepper

Preheat the oven to 160°C/325°F/Gas Mark 3. Heat the olive oil in a large cast iron casserole, lightly season the pork pieces with a little sea salt, then brown them well over a medium heat. Remove the pork from the pan and add the onion, carrots, leek and garlic. Reduce the heat to low and sauté the vegetables for about 5 minutes, until they have softened. Return the pork to the pan, stir in the flour and pour in the cider. Leave it to bubble for 1 minute, then add the stock or water. Tuck in the herbs and bring to the boil. Season with a touch more sea salt and a good grinding of black pepper and cover tightly with a lid or foil. Transfer the dish to the oven and cook for 1 hour.

Take the casserole from the oven and remove the lid. Being careful not to burn your fingers, lay the potato slices over the top of the stew, overlapping them as you go. When the surface is completely covered, brush the potatoes with the melted butter and cover the casserole again. Return it to the oven for 30 minutes. Remove the lid and give the pie a final blast for 15–20 minutes to brown the potatoes.

Chicken and Leek Pie

The most important aspect of a good chicken pie is the sauce. There's nothing worse than a sea of watery juices at the bottom of the bowl with bits of chicken and herbs bobbing about. Your sauce should be well flavoured and thick enough to coat the meat. Also, don't be tempted to use chicken breasts for this. The leaner meat tends to dry out, even when poached, and has nowhere near as much flavour as the thighs.

SERVES 4

1kg chicken thighs
1 small onion, chopped
1 carrot, chopped
4 leeks, trimmed and sliced (reserve the trimmings)
2 garlic cloves, peeled
1 bay leaf
a sprig of thyme
70g unsalted butter
50g plain flour
2 sprigs of tarragon, chopped
400g ready-made puff pastry
1 organic egg, beaten with a dash of milk
sea salt and freshly ground black pepper

Put the chicken thighs in a large, stainless steel saucepan with the onion, carrot, some of the dark green leek trimmings, garlic and herbs and pour in 600ml cold water. Season with a pinch of sea salt and bring slowly to the boil over a medium heat. Skim off any foamy scum that rises to the surface, then turn the heat down low to poach the thighs. This should take around 15–20 minutes. To check that they are done, insert a skewer next to the bone; if the juices run out clear, they're ready. Now remove the thighs from the pan and leave until cool enough to handle. Peel off the skin and pick the meat from the bone, keeping the meat from each thigh in 1 or 2 chunks. Place the meat in a bowl, then put the skin and bones back into the pot with the vegetables and simmer for 20 minutes – this stock will be the basis of your sauce. As the chicken skin holds a fair bit of fat, leave the stock to sit for 5 minutes, by which time the fat will have risen to the surface. Ladle it off and strain the stock into a large jug.

While all this is going on, melt 20g of the butter in a pan and add the leeks. Cover and cook over a low heat until the leeks have softened. Melt the remaining butter in a separate pan and stir in the flour. Cook gently for 1 minute and then remove from the heat. Gradually mix in the warm stock, stirring all the time so it doesn't become lumpy. Return the pan to the heat and simmer for 10 minutes, until the sauce has thickened. Remove from the heat, stir in the chicken, leeks and chopped tarragon, then season to taste with salt and pepper. Pour the filling into a 1-litre pie dish.

Preheat the oven to 200°C/400°F/Gas Mark 6. On a lightly floured board, roll out the pastry until it is a little larger than the pie dish and leave it to rest while the filling cools a little.

Brush the rim of the dish with a little of the beaten egg and lay the pastry over it. Press the edges of the pastry on to the dish with the tines of a fork, trim away any excess and cut a

small hole in the centre; this will let out the steam while it is cooking. Brush the pie lid with beaten egg and then place the pie on the middle shelf of the oven. Bake for 5 minutes, turn the temperature down to 180°C/350°F/Gas Mark 4 and continue cooking for 15–20 minutes, until the pastry is crisp and brown.

165   BAR MEALS

Gypsy Eggs
(Huevos a la Flamenca)

This may not be a gastropub classic in the broadest sense but it is a classic dish from the first of its kind, the Eagle. This is the type of food that epitomises what the Eagle is all about: simple, earthy and really, really tasty. It's also a sort of 'smash and grab' meal, using whatever kind of cured sausages you have to hand, so you needn't follow the recipe slavishly. If you have no ham, use some extra chorizo. Don't much like morcilla? Then leave it out and try another sausage. The possibilities are almost endless.

SERVES 4

2 tablespoons olive oil
100g serrano ham, chopped
100g chorizo, chopped
1 onion, diced
2 garlic cloves, crushed
1 teaspoon paprika, preferably Spanish sweet pimento
800g canned tomatoes, chopped
150g peas or broad beans, or both (frozen is fine)
100ml light chicken stock or water
350g potatoes, peeled and diced into 1cm cubes
100g morcilla sausage, chopped
8 organic eggs
sea salt and freshly ground black pepper

Heat the olive oil in a heavy-based saucepan and add the ham and chorizo. Sauté over a medium heat for 5 minutes, until they are beginning to crisp and the chorizo has given up most of it orange fat. Remove from the pan with a slotted spoon and set aside. Add the onion, garlic and paprika to the pan and cook over a low heat until the onion has softened. Tip in the tomatoes, peas or beans, stock or water and potatoes and bring to a simmer. Cover and cook over a low heat for 10–15 minutes, until the potatoes are tender.

Preheat the oven to 200°C/400°F/Gas Mark 6. Return the ham and chorizo to the pan and stir in the morcilla, being careful not to break up the delicate sausage. Warm through and season with sea salt and black pepper.

Divide the mixture between 4 individual ovenproof dishes. Make 2 little indentations in each portion and break the eggs into them. Bake on the middle shelf of the oven for 8–10 minutes, until the egg whites have just set.

Lancashire Hot Pot

I must confess that this is a dish I don't make very often, only because I have a weakness for my gran's lamb and barley stew (see page 172), but I do thoroughly enjoy it on a chilly winter's evening. The first place I turn to when I have a penchant for hot pot is the Anchor and Hope in Waterloo. Though Jonathon Jones is not a native of Lancashire, he serves up an honest and traditional interpretation of this classic dish, right down to the pickled red cabbage. This is his version.

SERVES 4

60g unsalted butter
2 onions, sliced
2 tablespoons plain flour
1kg neck of lamb chops
6 lamb's kidneys, skinned, core removed, and diced
200ml lamb stock or light chicken stock
1kg King Edward potatoes, peeled and sliced into 2mm discs
1 bay leaf
a sprig of thyme
sea salt and freshly ground black pepper

For the pickled red cabbage
1 red cabbage
2 tablespoons sea salt
475ml malt vinegar
6 black peppercorns
2 bay leaves
6 cloves
1/2 cinnamon stick
1 red chilli
150g caster sugar

For the pickled cabbage, discard the outer leaves of the cabbage, cut it into quarters and remove the core. Shred the cabbage finely, put it in a colander and sprinkle over the sea salt. Leave for 2 hours, then rinse off the salt under cold running water. Pat the cabbage dry, then pack it into sterilised Kilner jars (for sterilising jars, see page 196). Put the vinegar, spices and sugar into a stainless steel pan and bring to the boil, stirring to dissolve the sugar. Simmer for 5 minutes, then remove from the heat and leave to infuse while it cools. Strain the vinegar into a clean pan, bring back to the boil and pour it over the cabbage. Seal the jars and leave in a cool, dry place overnight (the cabbage will keep well in the fridge for a month).

Preheat the oven to 150°C/300°F/Gas Mark 2. Melt 20g of the butter in a large, heavy-based saucepan, add the onions and sauté over a low heat for 5 minutes, until softened. Remove with a slotted spoon and place on a plate. Season the flour with a pinch of sea salt and a touch of pepper and lightly dust the chops with it. Melt another 20g butter in the pan and brown the chops in small batches, being careful not to singe the flour, then transfer them to a plate. Quickly fry the kidneys in the same pan, then remove them too. Pour in the stock and let it bubble for a minute, scraping the crusty bits from the bottom of the pan. Remove from the heat and set aside.

Melt the remaining butter. Place the potato slices in a wide bowl, season with sea salt and black pepper and pour over the melted butter. Mix together really well – you need to coat all the potato slices – then lay half of them in a large casserole dish. Lay the chops and kidneys over the potatoes and tuck in the bay and thyme, then pour over the warm stock. Cover the meat with the onions, followed by the remaining potato slices, arranged so they overlap. Cover the dish with a tight-fitting lid or foil and bake for $1^1/_2$ hours. Remove the lid and cook for a further 30 minutes, until the potato topping is golden brown. Serve immediately, with the pickled cabbage on the side.

Kedgeree

A Victorian breakfast dish whose origins can be traced back to the British Raj, this makes for a cracking light lunch. The way I've found myself often making it is as a kind of Indian pilaf. Early recipes omit any traditional Indian seasoning, preferring a pinch of cayenne or even a spoonful of English mustard. I think it's important to have a gentle curry flavour, so I use a mild Madras curry powder along with a handful of curry leaves. These can be found, often frozen, in Asian groceries. It's also possible to buy curry plants at garden centres, and no, the leaves don't pong of curry until they hit the heat.

SERVES 4

500g smoked haddock fillet
75g unsalted butter
1 onion, finely diced
2 garlic cloves, finely sliced
1 teaspoon cumin seeds
2 teaspoons mild curry powder
1 tablespoon curry leaves
200g basmati rice
150g frozen peas, thawed
4 organic eggs
lemon wedges, to serve
sea salt and freshly ground black pepper

Place the smoked haddock in a wide saucepan and cover it with 800ml water. Place the pan over a medium heat and slowly bring to a simmer. When the surface of the water just begins to ripple, take the pan from the heat and leave the haddock to cool down a little in the liquid. Strain the liquor into a jug. Skin the fish, very lightly flake the flesh and keep it aside.

Melt the butter in a heavy-based saucepan, add the onion and garlic and cook over a low heat until soft and translucent. Stir in the cumin seeds and curry powder, along with the curry leaves – they will pop when they hit the heat. Cook for 1 minute, then add the rice with a pinch of sea salt and a grinding of black pepper. Mix the rice around until it is coated with the buttery spices. Pour in the haddock poaching liquid, bring to a simmer, then cover with a tight-fitting lid and leave to cook over the lowest possible heat for 15 minutes, until the rice is tender.

Remove the lid and quickly fold in the flaked fish and the peas. Cover the pan and leave over a low heat for 5 minutes to warm everything through.

Meanwhile, bring a pan of water to the boil, add a small pinch of sea salt and place the eggs in the pan. Boil them for 8 minutes, then refresh under cold running water, but don't let the eggs cool completely – they should still be a tad warm inside. When they are cool enough to handle, carefully peel the eggs.

To serve, pile the kedgeree on to warm plates, halve the eggs and dot them over the top. Pass around the lemon wedges.

Neck of Lamb and Barley

This is an approximation of a stew my grandmother used to serve when we were small children. She always used neck chops but I find them a bit too fiddly. Even with the best butchering, you always seem to end up with small shards of bone at the bottom of the stew. I've updated her recipe a little to serve at the Fox and it positively flies out of the bar.

SERVES 6

100g pearl barley
50g unsalted butter
a touch of olive oil
1kg neck of lamb fillet, cut into 2cm discs
1 large onion, diced
2 carrots, diced
2 celery stalks, diced
2 garlic cloves, crushed
1 teaspoon tomato purée
200ml white wine
400ml light stock or water
1 bay leaf
a sprig of thyme
1 tablespoon Worcestershire sauce
2 tablespoons chopped parsley
sea salt and freshly ground black pepper

Preheat the oven to 160°C/325°F/Gas Mark 3. Rinse the barley under cold running water, then put it in a small pan. Barely cover it with cold water, bring to the boil and simmer for 10 minutes, then drain and set aside.

Melt the butter and olive oil in a large cast iron casserole. Lightly season the lamb with a little sea salt, then add it to the pan and brown over a medium heat, being careful not to burn the meat or the butter. Transfer the meat to a plate and set aside. Add the onion, carrots, celery and garlic to the pan and sauté over a medium heat for 8–10 minutes, until soft and golden. Return the lamb to the pan, stir in the tomato purée, then pour in the wine, letting it bubble for a minute. Add the drained barley, along with the stock or water, and bring to the boil. The liquid should cover the ingredients by about 2cm – if necessary, top it up with a little water. Tuck in the herbs, add another pinch of salt and a grinding of pepper, and cover the pan tightly with a lid or foil. Place on the middle shelf of the oven and cook for $1^1/_2$ hours or until the meat is tender. Check the casserole from time to time, as the barley has a habit of sucking up the cooking juices; if the stew looks as if it's drying out, administer a touch more water.

Remove the casserole from the oven and stir in the Worcestershire sauce and chopped parsley. Ladle into deep bowls and serve at once.

Sausage and Bean Casserole

Homely and comforting, this is the kind of dish I crave on a cold winter's evening. The beans you use here are at your discretion, though I prefer butterbeans, as I think they make the whole dish more substantial. It does take a bit of forward planning, as you will need to soak the beans in advance, but a little cheating is acceptable if it's a quick dinner you're after – canned beans will cut the cooking time in half.

SERVES 6

350g dried beans
2 bay leaves
a sprig of thyme
3 tablespoons olive oil
150g smoked streaky bacon, either lardons or sliced rashers
1 onion, diced
2 carrots, diced
1 celery stalk, diced
2 garlic cloves, crushed
12 fat butcher's sausages
2 teaspoons tomato purée
sea salt and freshly ground black pepper

Put the beans in a large bowl and add enough water to cover by at least 10cm. Leave to soak overnight.

The next day, drain the beans and rinse them in cold water. Put them in a pot and pour in enough fresh water to cover by 10cm. Bring to the boil, skim off any scum that forms on the surface, then add the bay and thyme. Turn the heat down low and simmer for 1–1½ hours, until the beans are soft. Season them with a good pinch of sea salt and pick out and discard the thyme stalks and bay leaves. Set the beans aside in their liquid.

Preheat the oven to 220°C/425°F/Gas Mark 7. Heat 2 tablespoons of the olive oil in a large cast iron casserole and gently sauté the bacon pieces over a medium heat until they have rendered some of their fat and are crisping up around the edges. Add the onion, carrots, celery and garlic, then cover and cook over a low heat until the vegetables have softened. Meanwhile, heat the remaining olive oil in a frying pan, add the sausages and brown them all over. Tip them into the casserole, add the tomato purée, then ladle in the beans and enough of their liquid just to cover. Bring to a simmer, season with sea salt and pepper, then put the casserole, uncovered, on the middle shelf of the oven. Bake for 25–30 minutes, until the pot is positively bubbling and the top has browned evenly.

Ham and Chicory Gratin

Endive and witlof are just two of the European names given to the pale, torpedo-shaped salad leaf we know as chicory. It's more often found in salad bowls during the colder months but, like its close cousin, radicchio, it is also superb as a cooked vegetable. Braised with butter and stock or cream, or in this case warmed under a blanket of cheesy white sauce, chicory loses much of its inherent bitterness. This is a classic recipe, adapted from one of Jane Grigson's. It makes an ideal light lunch or supper.

SERVES 6

juice of ¹/₂ lemon
1 teaspoon caster sugar
6 chicory heads
6 slices of ham
Dijon mustard
sea salt and freshly ground black pepper

For the sauce
2 tablespoons unsalted butter
2 tablespoons plain flour
300ml full-fat milk, warmed
300ml light chicken stock, warmed
60g Parmesan cheese, freshly grated

Bring a pan of water to the boil, season with a pinch of sea salt, the lemon juice and sugar, then plunge in the chicory. Bring quickly back to the boil, then turn the heat to medium and simmer for 10 minutes. Drain thoroughly and leave the chicory to cool a little while you get on with the sauce.

Melt the butter in a heavy-based saucepan and, just as it starts to bubble, whisk in the flour. Cook for a minute over a medium heat until it becomes pale golden and begins to give off a nutty aroma. Remove from the heat and gradually whisk in the warm milk, stirring constantly to prevent it becoming lumpy. Place the sauce back on the heat and slowly whisk in the stock. Bring to a simmer, stirring all the time, then turn the heat as low as possible and let the sauce bubble gently for 15 minutes. Stir in all but 10g of the Parmesan, season to taste and keep warm.

Preheat the oven to 200°C/400°F/Gas Mark 6. Liberally butter a gratin dish. Now spread each slice of ham with about half a tablespoon of mustard and wrap it around a head of chicory. Place the chicory side by side in the gratin dish – it should be a snug fit – and pour over the sauce. Sprinkle over the remaining Parmesan and bake for 20–25 minutes, until the sauce is bubbling and the gratin has a lovely brown top.

Macaroni, Porcini and Parmesan Cheese

This is a twist on your everyday, standard macaroni cheese. Not that there's anything wrong with the conventional Cheddar sauce but I love the mushrooms here, particularly the dried porcini, which give the dish a strong, earthy flavour. Using Parmesan and Fontina, an oozy, semi-soft cow's milk cheese from the north of Italy, gives a nod to the macaroni's Italian roots.

SERVES 4

400g macaroni
a little olive oil
70g unsalted butter
1 onion, finely diced
300g flat mushrooms, sliced
25g dried porcini mushrooms, soaked in a little warm water for 10 minutes, then drained
50g plain flour
750ml full-fat milk, warmed
50g Fontina cheese, grated
80g Parmesan cheese, freshly grated
sea salt and freshly ground black pepper

Preheat the oven to 180°C/350°F/Gas Mark 4. Fill your largest pot with water, add a teaspoon of sea salt and bring to a rolling boil. Pour in the macaroni, stirring while you pour to stop the pasta sticking to the pan. Most brands recommend a cooking time of 12–13 minutes but as the pasta will be baked with the cheese here, it will need only about 8 minutes' boiling. When the time is up, drain the pasta, refresh it under cold running water, then rub through a little olive oil and leave to one side.

Melt 20g of the butter in a small saucepan, add the onion with a pinch of sea salt and cook, covered, over a low heat for 5 minutes, until soft and translucent. Add the flat mushrooms to the pan, cover again and cook for 5 minutes, until the mushrooms have wilted. Stir in the drained porcini, season to taste and set aside.

Melt the remaining butter in a separate pan. When it is just beginning to bubble, quickly stir in the flour. Cook over a low heat for 1 minute, until the mixture is golden and gives off a nice nutty aroma. Remove the pan from the heat and pour in half the milk, thoroughly mixing as you go to prevent lumps. Gradually stir in the rest of the milk, then return the sauce to a low heat and simmer gently for 5 minutes, until it begins to thicken. Now add all the Fontina and half the Parmesan and allow the cheese to melt into the sauce over a low heat. Tip in the mushrooms and check the sauce for seasoning; it may call for a touch more sea salt and a grinding of black pepper.

Combine the sauce with the pasta and pour them into a liberally buttered baking dish. Scatter over the remaining Parmesan and bake on the middle shelf of the oven for 25–30 minutes, until the cheese is bubbling and the top is crisp and brown.

Faggots and Mash

This recipe comes from Samantha Waterhouse, my colleague at the Fox. Samantha's parents and grandparents ran pubs in both the East End of London and the English countryside. By all accounts, Sam's grandfather was a fabulous cook. Luckily for us at the Fox, he passed down many a recipe to her, which in turn, she brought along to the Fox. She says of this recipe:

'My late Grandfather Percy loved this dish. We always ate it with mushy peas and mash. Faggots don't appear very often in pubs and this is my Foxy adaptation. Whenever we make them, they fly out of the door!'

SERVES 6

50g unsalted butter
a splash of vegetable oil
1 onion, diced
2 leeks, diced
2 carrots, diced
300g minced pork belly
100g smoked streaky bacon, diced
250g pig's liver, finely diced
250g pig's kidneys, skinned, core removed, and finely diced
a few sage leaves
a few sprigs of thyme
a pinch of ground mace
a pinch of ground allspice
300ml chicken or pork stock
100g fresh breadcrumbs
12 Savoy cabbage leaves, from the outside of the cabbage
100g caul fat
sea salt and freshly ground black pepper

Heat the butter and oil in a heavy-based pan, add the onion, leeks and carrots, then cover with a tight-fitting lid and cook for about 10 minutes, until the vegetables are soft. Add the minced pork belly and cook until sealed all over. Add the bacon, liver and kidneys and cook for a further 5 minutes. Season with salt and pepper, add the herbs and spices and pour in the stock. Bring to a simmer, then cover and leave over the lowest possible heat to braise for about an hour, until the meat is tender and the liquid has reduced by half. Mix in the breadcrumbs and leave to cool overnight – the mixture is easier to handle when cold.

Preheat the oven to 180°C/350°F/Gas Mark 4. Bring a large pot of water to a rolling boil and throw in the cabbage leaves. Cook for 3–5 minutes, until they are soft, then drain and quickly refresh them under cold running water. Drain again and spread out on a tea towel to dry.

Take a handful of the meat mixture, form it into an egg-sized ball and place it in the middle of one of the cabbage leaves. Wrap the leaf around the meat like a blanket. Wrap up the rest of the meat in the same way, then lay out the caul fat on a flat surface. Cut it into 12 squares and wrap the faggots in it, pulling the fat right around them to cover them tightly.

Put the faggots in an ovenproof dish, add a splash of water (about 100ml) and place on the middle shelf of the oven. Bake for 20–25 minutes, until the caul fat is golden brown. Serve with mushy peas, buttery mashed potatoes and the cooking juices.

Steak and Kidney Pudding

What could be more English than steak and kidney pudding? The delicious, old-fashioned union of beef with its flavoursome offal is a firm pub favourite, and surprisingly easy to make. Traditionally the pudding is put together by layering the raw ingredients in the pastry case and topping it up with water or stock. I think the filling is better if made in advance, as with any good pie. And, like any fine stew, the flavour and texture are always better after a day's rest. Once the filling is cooked and the pudding assembled, the steaming time can be cut from 5 to 2 hours.

SERVES 6

80g unsalted butter
2 onions, diced
250g mushrooms, sliced
1kg stewing steak, cut into 2cm cubes
500g ox kidneys, skinned, core removed, and cut into 2cm cubes
2 tablespoons plain flour
200ml red wine
400ml beef stock or water
2 bay leaves
a sprig of thyme
sea salt and freshly ground black pepper

For the suet pastry
350g self-raising flour
180g suet

Preheat the oven to 160°C/325°F/Gas Mark 3. Melt half the butter in a cast iron casserole and add the onions with a pinch of sea salt. Sauté over a low heat for 5 minutes, until they are beginning to soften and have browned slightly. Add the mushrooms and cook for 3–4 minutes, until they have softened too. Remove with a slotted spoon and set aside. Add the remaining butter to the pan and then introduce the steak and kidneys. Raise the heat a little and fry the meat until it is sealed and browned. Return the onions and mushrooms to the pan and add the flour, stirring until it has all been absorbed. Pour over the red wine and let it bubble for 1 minute. Now add the stock or water and the herbs and season with sea salt and a grinding of black pepper. Cover the casserole with a tight-fitting lid and cook on the middle shelf of the oven for 1½ hours, until the meat is almost tender. Remove from the oven and leave to cool completely.

To make the suet pastry, sift the flour into a wide mixing bowl, add a pinch of sea salt and a good grind of black pepper, then mix in the suet with the blade of a knife until it is incorporated. Pour in some cold water, a drop at a time, until the flour and suet begin to come together to form a ball. Turn it out of the bowl on to a floured board and knead lightly, just until soft and pliable. Cut off a quarter of the dough and set that aside for the lid. Roll out the rest into a circle large enough to line a 1.3 litre pudding basin. Lightly butter the basin and fit the pastry in, pressing it right on to the surface and leaving 1cm of pastry hanging over the side. Fill the basin with the cooled stew, then roll out the rest of the pastry into a circle to make the lid. Dampen the overhanging pastry, pop the lid on top and press the edges together firmly to make a seal. Cover the pudding with a double layer

of foil with a pleat in the centre – this will allow it to rise during steaming. Secure the foil with string.

Put the pudding in a metal steamer placed over a pan of simmering water – or, if you don't have a steamer, place it on an upturned plate in a large saucepan and pour boiling water into the pan until it comes two thirds of the way up the sides of the bowl. Cover with a tight-fitting lid and simmer for 2 hours, topping up the pan with more boiling water every once in a while to make sure it never boils dry.

Carefully remove the basin from the pan, take off the foil lid and run a knife around the rim of the bowl. Unmould the pudding on to a warm plate and serve straight away.

Roast pumpkin

Wild mushroo

Clams, white

Smoked hadd

Cod & turkey

Bar Snacks

A Pint of Prawns and Mayonnaise
Stilton and Spring Onion Tart
Swiss Chard and Feta Pie
Rump Steak Sandwich
Salt Beef Sandwich
Scotch Eggs
Sausage Rolls
Cornish Pasties
Ploughman's Lunch

A Pint of Prawns and Mayonnaise

This is not so much a recipe as a few simple instructions on how to put together a snack that is enjoyed in pubs and bars the world over. The most important thing is the shopping: buy the best and freshest prawns you can find. I go for the larger 'green', or raw, prawns in the shell. The best specimens are firm, with a good bright colour, and smell faintly of the sea. Never buy prawns with black heads or legs – a telltale sign of age. Frozen raw prawns make an acceptable alternative to fresh ones. Thaw them slowly in the fridge on a layer of kitchen paper and cook them as soon as possible.

Allow 8 large raw prawns per person

The ideal cooking liquid for all shellfish is seawater but heavily salted fresh water makes a good alternative. Fill your largest saucepan with water, adding 50g sea salt to each litre of water. Bring to a rolling boil and drop in the prawns. When the water has come back to the boil, lower the heat to medium and simmer until they change colour; this should take 2–3 minutes. Check the prawns by lightly squeezing one just under its head – it should be firm but not too solid. Remove the cooked prawns from the water and leave them to drain thoroughly. Serve warm or at room temperature with a pot of mayonnaise (see page 230) and a loaf of crusty white bread.

Stilton and Spring Onion Tart

Quiche, flan, tart, call it what you want. Though it is traditionally seen as the 'ladies' or vegetarian option on the gastropub menu, there is nothing dainty about this tart, and it's certainly not for the fainthearted. Punchy, strong flavours are complemented by crisp, short, buttery pastry. A Colston Bassett Stilton with its lively, salty blue veins and creamy overtones is essential but be warned: a little Stilton goes a long way here.

SERVES 4–6

3 organic eggs
180ml double cream
1 small bunch of spring onions, finely sliced
100g Stilton cheese
sea salt and freshly ground black pepper

For the pastry
300g plain flour
a pinch each of sea salt and nutmeg
150g fridge-cold unsalted butter
1 organic egg
90ml milk

First make the pastry. Sift the flour into a bowl, season with the sea salt and nutmeg and mix it around to combine. Coarsely grate the butter into the bowl and, using your fingertips, lightly rub it into the flour until the mixture has the texture of fine breadcrumbs. Make a well in the centre, break in the egg and pour in the milk. Using a table knife, work the egg and milk into the flour, scraping the sides and bottom of the bowl, until the dough has formed into a rough lump. Tip the lump on to a lightly floured surface and roll it into a flat patty. Wrap in cling film and chill for about 30 minutes. Then roll it out into a circle large enough to fit a 24cm loose-bottomed tart tin. Press the pastry into the tin, making sure that it fits into the edges, then trim off the excess. Chill for 30 minutes.

Preheat the oven to 200°C/400°F/Gas Mark 6. Line the pastry case with baking paper and fill this with dried beans or, better still, ceramic baking beans, if you have them. Bake on the middle shelf of the oven for 15 minutes, then remove the paper and beans. Return the pastry case to the oven for another 5 minutes, until the base is lightly browned. A good tip is to brush the hot pastry with beaten egg and pop it back in the oven for another 2 minutes; this will completely seal the base and cover any hairline cracks.

For the filling, whisk together the eggs and cream and add the spring onions. Season with a touch of sea salt – remember that the cheese is quite strong – and a grinding of black pepper. Crumble the Stilton all over the base of the pastry case and pour over the eggy cream. Place the tart on the middle shelf of the oven, turn the heat down to 180°C/350°F/Gas Mark 4 and bake for 20 minutes, until the filling is set. Serve warm with a green salad.

Swiss Chard and Feta Pie

This is a recipe that I've taken with me from one establishment to another, starting out in Sydney, then all the way to the Fox. It's my mother's version of spinach and Feta pie – need I say more...

SERVES 8

1 bunch of Swiss chard, weighing around 1kg
1 bunch of spring onions, sliced
250g Feta cheese, crumbled
125g Cheddar cheese, grated
100g unsalted butter, melted
½ packet of filo pastry
6 organic eggs
sea salt and freshly ground black pepper

Wash the chard, cut off the white stalks and either spin the leaves in a salad spinner or dry them with a tea towel. Finely slice the stalks and shred the leaves.

Put the chard in a bowl with the spring onions, Feta and grated Cheddar, then add a good grind of black pepper and a touch of sea salt – remember, the Feta is quite salty. Mix everything together well with your hands.

Grease a 20 x 30cm baking dish with a little of the melted butter and line it with a sheet of filo pastry. It needs to hang over the sides a little, so use 2 sheets if necessary. Brush the filo with melted butter, then add another layer. Repeat with 2 more layers of pastry. Arrange the chard mixture on top. Beat the eggs until they are frothy and add a small grinding of black pepper to them. Pour the eggs evenly over the chard. Cover with 2 more layers of filo, as before, brushing each layer with melted butter. Fold the sides in and brush the top with more butter.

Preheat the oven to 180°C/350°F/Gas Mark 4. Using a sharp knife, slice through the top layer of the pastry, cutting it into even-sized squares; this will let the steam out during cooking. Bake on the middle shelf of the oven for 45 minutes or until the pastry is crisp and a light golden brown. Leave to rest for 10 minutes – as the cheese cools, the pie will set a little further. Serve warm or at room temperature, with a green salad.

Rump Steak Sandwich

No bar menu is complete without a juicy steak sandwich and the Eagle's Bife Ana is one of the best. Before I even thought about working there I was a regular diner, and the Bife Ana was my first choice for a quick lunch. It isn't the traditional Portuguese sandwich of that name, which is made with pork escalope, but the type David Eyre, co-founder of The Eagle, enjoyed as a child in his native Mozambique. I must have made thousands of these in my time at the Eagle and they still can't be bettered.

SERVES 2

500g rump steak, thinly sliced
2 large, crusty rolls
2 tablespoons olive oil
Cos lettuce
sea salt and freshly ground black pepper

For the marinade
1 onion, thinly sliced
1 garlic clove, thinly sliced
1 small red chilli, finely sliced
1 bay leaf, broken up
1 tablespoon chopped parsley
2 tablespoons red wine
3 tablespoons olive oil

Mix all the ingredients for the marinade together in a wide bowl. Add the slices of steak and leave to marinate for 2 hours or so – not much longer, or the wine will draw too much liquid from the meat. Remove the steaks from the marinade, let them sit on pieces of kitchen paper for a few minutes to absorb the excess moisture, then drain the liquid and keep to one side.

Warm the rolls in a low oven. Heat the olive oil in a heavy-based frying pan until it is very hot, almost on the point of smoking, then put the steaks in the pan. Fry them quickly on each side until sealed – it should take less than a minute per side – then transfer them to a warm plate. Add the onion, garlic and chilli from the marinade to the pan with a pinch of sea salt and fry for 1 minute, until soft and lightly browned. Pour in the marinade and let it bubble until reduced by half.

Slice the rolls in half and lay a couple of Cos lettuce leaves on the bottom of each one. Place the steaks on top, season lightly with sea salt and black pepper and pour over the marinade. Pop on the top of the roll and squish it down hard. Eat immediately, with plenty of napkins on one side to help mop up the juices.

Salt Beef Sandwich

As the Fox is situated on the fringes of the East End, we thought it only appropriate to offer a classic salt beef sandwich on the bar menu all year round. I buy superb organic beef brisket from my butcher, Barry Hadden, in Essex, then pop down to nearby Brick Lane, the home of the salt beef sandwich, to source the dill pickled cucumbers and great rye bread.

The amount of beef in this recipe may seem rather a lot but it keeps perfectly well, covered with its liquid in the fridge, for 4 or 5 days. Apart from making a fine sandwich, it also provides the basis of an excellent supper with a bowl of mashed potatoes and some carrots.

3kg boned brisket
2 carrots, peeled and halved
1 onion, peeled and halved
1 leek, halved
2 celery stalks, halved
1 teaspoon black peppercorns

For the brine
2.5 litres water
500g coarse sea salt
250g brown sugar
2 bay leaves
a sprig each of rosemary and thyme
$1^{1}/_{2}$ teaspoons juniper berries

To serve
rye and caraway bread
American mustard
dill pickled cucumbers (bought or home-made – see page 198)

To make the brine, put all the ingredients in a pan and bring to the boil, stirring to dissolve the salt and sugar. Leave to cool completely.

Cut the brisket into manageable chunks of around a kilo each and put them in a container large enough to hold them and the brine comfortably. Pour the brine over the brisket and weight the meat down with a plate, or something heavy enough to keep the meat submerged. Cover the container tightly and leave it in the fridge or a cool place for 1 week.

Take the meat from the brine and soak it in clean water for about 12 hours or overnight. Now put the meat into a large, wide pan, cover with fresh water and add the carrots, onion, leek, celery and peppercorns. Bring to a simmer, then turn the heat down low and cook for 2–$2^{1}/_{2}$ hours, until the meat is tender. Never let it boil or the meat can become tough.

To serve, cut the warm meat into slices a couple of millimetres thick, then pile it between slices of rye and caraway bread with a liberal squeeze of American mustard. Serve with dill pickled cucumbers.

Scotch Eggs

Portable and delicious, the Scotch egg isn't only for picnics. It's also a great 'stand at the bar with a pint' kind of snack. You could ask your butcher for finely minced pork belly to wrap around the eggs but I prefer my cheating version. I buy good butcher's sausages such as Lincolnshire or Cumberland or even pork and leek, and squeeze the insides for the savoury casing.

MAKES 6

8 organic eggs
300g good sausages
50g plain flour
200g fresh breadcrumbs
vegetable oil for deep-frying
sea salt and freshly ground black pepper

Bring a pan of lightly salted water to the boil and lower in 6 of the eggs. Cook for 7 minutes, then drain and leave under cold running water for about 3 minutes to cool completely. Carefully peel them and set aside.

Slice through the sausage casing with a sharp knife and turn out the sausage meat on to a board. Divide it into 6, roll each piece into a ball, then squash it flat.

Now you need 3 bowls. In one, whisk the remaining eggs. In the second, mix the flour with a pinch of sea salt and a grinding of black pepper. Put the breadcrumbs into the third.

Dust the boiled eggs in the flour, shake off any excess and set them aside. Now take a flattened sausagemeat patty in one hand and place an egg in the middle, then carefully fold the meat around the egg, making sure there are no gaps. Do the same with the rest of the eggs. Roll the eggs in the flour again, dip them in beaten egg and then roll them through the breadcrumbs to coat.

In a deep-fat fryer or a deep saucepan, heat some vegetable oil to 180°C/350°F (if you don't have a thermometer, drop a small piece of bread into the oil; if it turns golden within the minute, the oil is just right). Fry the eggs in batches, 2 or 3 at a time, for 8 minutes, until crisp and golden. Drain on kitchen paper and serve warm or cold.

Sausage Rolls

Another great bar snack, with many of the versatile attributes of the Scotch egg; small, tasty and great with a pint. Again, I think the meat is important when making a good sausage roll, so avoid pappy pink cheap mince and go for a good, though not too whacky, sausage. A highly seasoned English sausage such as Cumberland or Lincolnshire is best – chorizo or merguez are just too weird for this humble snack.

MAKES 8

400g good sausages
350g puff pastry
1 organic egg
sea salt

Preheat the oven to 220°C/425°F/Gas Mark 7. Slit the sausage casing with a sharp knife and turn the meat out on to a board. Pull all the sausage meat together and then divide it into 4.

Cut your pastry slab into quarters and roll one piece out into a 20 x 10cm rectangle on a lightly floured surface. Roll one piece of meat into a sausage the length of the pastry and place it on the edge. Lightly beat the egg with a tiny pinch of sea salt, then brush it over the opposite edge of the pastry. Roll the sausage up in the pastry and seal the edge by pressing it on to the underneath of the roll. Cut the roll in half and score the top with a knife. Repeat with the remaining pastry and sausagemeat to make 8 sausage rolls.

Put the sausage rolls on a baking tray lined with greaseproof paper and leave to rest for 15 minutes. Brush the tops with beaten egg and then bake on the middle shelf of the oven for 5 minutes. Reduce the temperature to 180°C/350°F/Gas Mark 4 and continue cooking for 15 minutes, until the pastry is golden. Serve warm, with tomato ketchup.

Cornish Pasties

Though not necessarily classic gastropub fare, a Cornish pasty easily fits into the 'pie and a pint' approach of the bar menu. The quantities for these simple turnovers can be easily doubled for entertaining a crowd, and it's good to know that they also freeze well.

MAKES 4

200g beef skirt or chuck, roughly chopped
1 onion, diced
1 large potato, peeled and diced
$1/_2$ medium swede, peeled and diced
1 organic egg, beaten with a drop of milk
sea salt and freshly ground black pepper

For the shortcrust pastry
220g plain flour
100g fridge-cold lard, cut into 1cm dice
$1/_2$ teaspoon sea salt
2 tablespoons water

To make the pastry, sift the flour into a wide mixing bowl and add the lard and salt. Rub the fat into the flour with your fingertips until the mixture resembles fine breadcrumbs, then pour in the water and mix to form a firm dough. Turn out on to a floured surface and knead lightly for a minute or so, until smooth. Wrap in cling film and chill for 30 minutes.

Place the beef, onion, potato and swede in a bowl and season with sea salt and black pepper. Preheat the oven to 200°C/400°F/Gas Mark 6.

Divide the pastry into 4 balls and roll them into discs about 14cm across. Trim the edges, using a saucer as a template. Share the filling between the pastry discs, brush the edges with beaten egg and fold them over into the traditional pasty shape. Crimp the edges, then brush the pasties with more beaten egg.

Place the pasties on a baking tray lined with greaseproof paper and bake on the middle shelf of the oven for 35–40 minutes, until golden brown and crisp. Serve hot or cold.

Ploughman's Lunch

It's possible that the notion of the ploughman's lunch dates back to the eighteenth century. Its first known mention in print is in the memoirs of Sir Walter Scott, the prolific Scottish writer, where it is described as either a sandwich or a boiled beef dinner. Another popular view is that the ploughman's consisted of whatever morsels of food could be found in the kitchen, tied in a handkerchief and taken into the fields by rural workers for their midday meal. It found its way into the Oxford English Dictionary in the 1970s, describing the familiar snack seen in pubs around the country today. There it is attributed to the British Milk Marketing Board as a ploy to shift one of their core products – cheese. But whatever its history, the ploughman's is essentially simple lunchtime pub grub.

The foundation for any good ploughman's is the cheese. I prefer it made with a traditional British cheese, and here in London I'm lucky enough to have Neal's Yard Dairy on my doorstep. From them I would choose a mature regional cheese, such as a tangy Cheddar, a creamy, crumbly Lancashire, a flaky-textured Cheshire or an earthy, lactic Caerphilly. To give the plate a festive feel around Christmas time, I'd go for the king of blue cheese, Colston Bassett Stilton.

Crusty white or brown bread should be the next thing to go on the plate. Find a good sourdough loaf and slice it into doorstep wedges. Next to the bread sits a pat of unsalted butter, to be generously slathered over the surface. A crisp apple, a blob of chutney and a 'wally' – a pickled gherkin in east London parlance – should finish it all off.

Any gastropub worth its salt will make its own condiments. At the Fox we have a corner of the kitchen filled with jars of pickles, chutneys and preserves for our ploughman's and terrines. Below are a few of my favourites.

Green Tomato Chutney

This is the chutney to make at the beginning and end of the tomato season. The first English green tomatoes appear in the springtime, pale and acidic from the lack of sunshine, and the second batch comes in around the end of September – the small, late fruit that misses out on an Indian summer.

MAKES 2.5KG

600ml red wine vinegar
4 tablespoons mustard seeds
500g soft light brown sugar
2 tablespoons sea salt
2kg green tomatoes, sliced
200g raisins
400g apples, peeled, cored and sliced
4 garlic cloves, crushed
2 large onions, sliced

Put the vinegar, mustard seeds, sugar and salt into a large, stainless steel pan and bring slowly to the boil. Add the tomatoes, raisins, apples, garlic and onions and bring back to

the boil. Turn the heat down low and leave the chutney to simmer for about 1 hour, stirring occasionally, until quite thick and jammy.

Meanwhile, sterilise your jars. Preheat the oven to 140°C/275°F/Gas Mark 1. Wash the jars in hot, soapy water and then give them a good rinse under the hot tap. Being careful not to touch the insides of the jars, place them upside down in the oven and leave to dry for 1–2 minutes. Remove the jars from the oven. Fill them while they and the chutney are still hot and seal tightly. Leave the chutney in a cool, dark place for 1 month before use.

Rhubarb Chutney

This recipe comes courtesy of Harry Lester. In the early days of the Fox, we dabbled with many a recipe for chutneys and pickles before landing on this one, which was particularly suited to the rhubarb from his mother's Peckham allotment.

MAKES ABOUT 3KG

1kg rhubarb, roughly chopped
450g onions, finely sliced
juice and grated zest of 2 oranges
850ml wine vinegar or malt vinegar
1kg soft light brown sugar
1 tablespoon allspice berries
1 tablespoon mustard seeds
1 tablespoon peppercorns (black or white)

Place the rhubarb, onions, orange juice and zest, vinegar and sugar in a large, stainless steel pan. Tie the spices in a piece of muslin and tuck them into the fruit. Place the pan over a medium heat and bring slowly to the boil. Turn the heat down low and leave the mixture on a steady simmer for about 1½ hours, stirring occasionally, until thick and pulpy. Sterilise your jars as for Green Tomato Chutney (see above). Pour the hot chutney into the jars and seal immediately. Store in a cool, dry place for 1 month before opening.

Pickled Quince

Hardly conventional with a ploughman's, but I love pickled quince with creamy, crumbly cheeses such as Caerphilly or Lancashire. The lightly spiced fruit also sits perfectly next to a slab of roast pork or a slice of cold ham.

MAKES ABOUT 3KG

6 ripe quinces
juice of 1 lemon
1.2 litres red wine vinegar
900g caster sugar
1 teaspoon cloves
1 teaspoon allspice berries
1 red chilli

Peel the quinces, cut them into quarters and remove the core. Place them in a bowl of water acidulated with the lemon juice to stop them discolouring. Bring the vinegar, sugar and spices to the boil in a heavy-based stainless steel pan, stirring to dissolve the sugar. Drain the quince, add them to the pan and simmer for 15–20 minutes, until they are tender and a deep red colour.

Sterilise your jars as for Green Tomato Chutney (see opposite). Leave the quince to cool a little in the liquid before carefully removing them with a slotted spoon and putting them in the jars. Put the pan back over a high heat and boil the liquid for 10 minutes to reduce it a little, then pour the hot syrup over the fruit. Seal the jars straight away and leave for a month in a cool, dry place before opening.

Piccalilli

Piccalilli is an indispensable condiment in my kitchen. I use it for everything from simple ham sandwiches to raised pies and fish dishes. Try it with Smoked Mackerel Pâté (see page 52) – it's sensational.

MAKES 1.5KG

1.5 litres boiling water
150g sea salt
300g cauliflower florets
200g small shallots, peeled
200g cucumber, peeled, seeded and cut into 2cm dice
200g courgettes, cut into 2cm dice
200g runner beans, cut into 2cm lengths
600ml malt vinegar
100g soft light brown sugar
2 teaspoons allspice berries
30g plain flour
1 tablespoon English mustard powder
1 tablespoon ground turmeric
2 teaspoons ground ginger

Pour the boiling water into a wide bowl, add the sea salt and stir until dissolved. Leave to cool.

Add all the vegetables to the bowl, weight them down with a plate, making sure they are completely submerged, and leave in a cool place for 12 hours or overnight.

The next day, put the vinegar, sugar and allspice into a large, stainless steel saucepan and bring to the boil. Simmer over a medium heat for 10 minutes. Meanwhile, drain the vegetables in a colander. Sterilise your jars as for Green Tomato Chutney (see opposite).

Pick out the cauliflower and shallots, add them to the pan and simmer for 5 minutes. Add the remaining vegetables and simmer for a further 4 minutes; they should still have a bit of crunch to them. Remove the vegetables with a slotted spoon directly into the hot sterilised jars and set aside.

Mix together the flour, mustard powder, turmeric and ginger in a bowl and add a ladleful of the hot vinegar – enough to make a smooth paste. Pour the paste into the pan of vinegar, stirring all the time, and simmer for 10 minutes, until the sauce is thick. Pour the sauce into the jars and seal immediately. Leave for a month in a cool, dark place to mature.

'Wallys' or Dill Pickled Cucumbers

The wally, or sweet and sour cucumber, is a traditional East End delicacy. I serve them with salt beef sandwiches (see page 188) as well as with ploughman's. They also give piquancy and extra crunch to salsa verde and tartare sauce. I've adapted this recipe from one in *The Book of Jewish Food* by Claudia Roden (Viking, 1997).

ENOUGH FOR TWO 2-LITRE JARS

1kg small or pickling cucumbers
1 bunch of dill
1 teaspoon peppercorns
1.5 litres water
70g sea salt
2 tablespoons white wine vinegar

Wash the cucumbers and dry them thoroughly. Sterilise two 2-litre jars as for Green Tomato Chutney (see pages 194-5). Put the cucumbers upright in the jars with the dill and peppercorns, making sure they're packed quite tightly. Put the water, salt and vinegar in a stainless steel pan, bring to the boil, then leave to cool. Pour the liquid over the cucumbers – they should be completely covered – then screw on the lids. Keep the pickles in a cool, dry place for 1 week before opening. Once opened, they will keep well for a month.

Pickled Shallots

The smaller of the alliums, shallots always seem to me to make a better pickle than onions. More subtle in flavour and easier to manoeuvre into your mouth, they are a perfect partner for your 'wally' on the ploughman's plate.

ENOUGH FOR A 1-LITRE JAR

450ml boiling water
50g sea salt
450g shallots, peeled
450ml malt vinegar
1 bay leaf
1 small red chilli
1 teaspoon allspice berries
1 teaspoon peppercorns

Pour the boiling water into a wide bowl, add the salt and stir until dissolved. Leave to cool, then tip in the shallots. Weight them down with a plate, making sure they are completely submerged, and leave in a cool place overnight.

The next day, bring the vinegar to the boil with the bay leaf, whole chilli and spices. Simmer for 5 minutes, then leave to cool. Sterilise your jars as for Green Tomato Chutney (see pages 194-5). Tightly pack the shallots into the jars, pour over the vinegar solution and screw on the lids. Leave in a cool, dry place for 1 month to mature before using.

Roast pumpkin

wild mushroo

clams, white

Smoked hadd

cod & parsley

Puddings

Prune and Almond Tart
Chocolate Pots
Iced Praline Parfait
Baked Custard and Quince
Peach Jelly
Peach Jelly Trifle
Baked Rice and Jam
Strawberry Shortcake
Raspberry Ripple Semifreddo
Sticky Toffee Pudding with Butterscotch Sauce
Black Forest Gâteau
Steamed Golden Syrup Pudding
Buttermilk Pudding
Lemon Tart
Crème Caramel
Rhubarb and Apple Crumble
Summer Pudding
Blood Orange Posset with Tuiles
Lemon Delicious
Treacle Tart

Prune and Almond Tart

Almond frangipane tarts are a great favourite and so simple to make. They are also possibly the most forgiving of tarts – the sweet oil from the almonds, combined with the generous amount of butter, melts slowly into the pastry shell during cooking and soaks up the juice from the fruit, ensuring that the pastry stays crisp. It's worth noting that you can change the fruit to suit the season – so, cherries in spring, peaches and nectarines in summer and pears and apples in the winter months. The only caveat is that the fruit must be ripe to extract the full flavour.

SERVES 6–8

300g pitted prunes
70g caster sugar
1 tea bag (your everyday type, not a fancy or scented kind)
250g whole blanched almonds
25g plain flour
3 organic eggs
250g unsalted butter
a little brandy or Armagnac

For the pastry
225g plain flour
50g caster sugar
115g fridge-cold unsalted butter, diced
1 organic egg
40ml cold milk

The first thing to do is to soak the prunes, preferably overnight. Place them in a bowl, sprinkle over 20g of the sugar and tuck in the tea bag. Pour over enough boiling water to cover the prunes by 2cm, then leave them to plump up in the liquid.

For the pastry, put the flour and sugar into a food processor and whiz until completely combined. Add the butter and pulse until it has just mixed in; you're looking for a fine breadcrumb texture. Add the egg and, with the machine running, pour in the milk. Stop the machine as soon as the pastry forms a ball. Scrape out the dough, pat it into a disc, then wrap in cling film and chill for 1 hour.

Roll out the pastry on a lightly floured board and use to line a 24cm loose-bottomed tart tin. Leave to rest in the fridge for an hour.

Preheat the oven to 180°C/350°F/Gas Mark 4. Prick the pastry base all over with a fork, cover with greaseproof paper and weight it down with dried beans, or ceramic baking beans if you have them. Bake on the middle shelf of the oven for 15 minutes, then remove the paper and beans. Return to the oven for 5 minutes, until the pastry base is firm and golden. Remove from the oven and leave to cool while you make the frangipane.

Whiz the almonds and the remaining sugar together in a food processor – a very noisy affair, this – until the almonds are finely chopped, though not too smooth. Add the flour, eggs and butter and process for half a minute more, until the mixture is creamy. Pour the frangipane into the cooked pastry case. Pick the prunes from the soaking liquid and shake off any excess moisture, then lightly push them into the frangipane.

Bake the tart for 30 minutes at 180°C/350°F/Gas Mark 4, then turn the oven down to 150°C/300°F/Gas Mark 2 and continue cooking for 10 minutes, until the tart is brown and the middle is just set but still a little springy.

Sprinkle a touch of brandy or Armagnac over the tart as it comes out of the oven. Leave to cool to room temperature before serving.

Chocolate Pots

The pudding list in most gastropubs is usually short and ahem... sweet. No more than 3 or 4 desserts are usually on offer, so the balance needs to be just right. I think most people would agree that no dessert menu is complete without a little chocolate, so I thought I should offer you these lovely pots. They're more like rich sponges than a mousse, so are not at all dense or overly sweet. They are best eaten on the day you make them – I like to serve them with a bowl of fresh raspberries.

SERVES 6

½ vanilla pod
175ml double cream
125g dark chocolate with 70 per cent cocoa solids, chopped
75ml milk
2 organic egg yolks
30g icing sugar

Preheat the oven to 140°C/275°F/Gas Mark 1. Slit the vanilla pod lengthways, scrape out the seeds, then put the pod and seeds in a small pan with the cream. Warm the cream, remove from the heat and leave to infuse for 30 minutes. In a separate pan, melt the chocolate in the milk over a gentle heat, then leave to the side to cool a little.

Whisk together the egg yolks and icing sugar, then pour in the chocolate milk and the cream. Mix together, pass the mixture through a sieve and pour into 6 ramekins. Place the ramekins in a baking tray and pour enough hot water into the tray to come half way up the sides of the ramekins. Bake for between 45 minutes and 1 hour, until the puddings are a little spongy and puffed up. Leave to cool for around 4 hours before serving.

Iced Praline Parfait

Such a simple yet impressive summer dessert, iced praline parfait is basically an icy nut and toffee log. It can be sliced with a warm knife into neat portions that look and taste fantastic, especially when served with poached apricots. If you haven't got the time or patience to make ice cream, this is the perfect (parfait) alternative.

SERVES 6

60g whole blanched almonds
60g hazelnuts
260g caster sugar
120ml water
3 organic egg whites
a pinch of sea salt
300ml double cream

Preheat the oven to 180°C/350°F/Gas Mark 4. Spread the almonds out on one baking tray and the hazelnuts on another and roast them for about 10 minutes, until golden and fragrant. Tip the hazelnuts into a clean tea towel and rub them vigorously to remove the skins, then lay both the almonds and hazelnuts on a lightly oiled baking tray.

Put the sugar and water in a heavy-based saucepan and heat, stirring, until the sugar has dissolved. Then boil, without stirring, over a high heat until it becomes deep brown and starts to give off a strong smell of caramel. You will have to work fast now, so carefully pour the boiling caramel over the nuts and then leave them in a cool place to set. Break the praline into chunks and pulse them in a food processor in 2 batches. The ideal texture for the parfait is a coarse, sandy praline with a small amount of nutty nuggets to get your teeth into.

Line an 800ml terrine mould or loaf tin with cling film. Whip the egg whites with the salt until they form stiff peaks. In another bowl, whip the cream to soft peaks. Carefully fold the praline into the whipped cream with a spatula until just combined, then fold in one third of the egg white. Now gently fold in the remaining whites and pour the mixture into the prepared mould. Cover and freeze for at least 12 hours, preferably overnight.

To serve, unmould the terrine on to a board, remove the cling film, and slice with a hot sharp knife.

Baked Custard and Quince

This version is a little lighter than traditional recipes for baked custard, as I prefer to use milk rather than cream. The milk gives it a silky, smooth texture – much less dense than cream-based versions – and each portion literally trembles on the plate before you dig in. I like to serve it with warm, spicy poached quince, whose richness and depth make it a perfect partner to the cool, milky custard.

SERVES 4

400ml water
100ml white wine
200g caster sugar
juice of $\frac{1}{2}$ lemon
1 vanilla pod
1 star anise
1 bay leaf
1 red chilli
4 quinces

For the custard
350ml full-fat milk
2 organic eggs
2 organic egg yolks
50g caster sugar

In a stainless steel pot, bring the water, wine, sugar and lemon juice to the boil, stirring until the sugar has dissolved. Halve the vanilla pod, keeping one half aside for the custard, then slit it down the middle and add it to the pot, along with the star anise, bay leaf and whole chilli.

Peel, quarter and core the quinces one at a time, adding the quarters to the pot as you go so they don't discolour. Cover the surface of the mixture with a circle of greaseproof paper and weight that down with a slightly smaller lid; this will keep the fruit completely submerged. Simmer for about 30 minutes, until the quince have turned slightly pink and are soft. Allow them to cool in the liquid.

Meanwhile, make the custard. Pour the milk into a pan. Slit the rest of the vanilla pod down the middle, scrape out the seeds, then add them with the pod to the milk. Warm the milk slightly, then remove from the heat and leave to infuse for 10 minutes. Preheat the oven to 150°C/350°F/Gas Mark 4.

Whisk together the eggs, egg yolks and sugar, then pour in the warm milk, stirring to combine. Pass the mixture through a sieve into an ovenproof dish and place the dish into a roasting tin of hot water; the water should come about two thirds of the way up the sides. Bake for around 1 hour, until the custard has a slight wobble in the middle about 2cm across. Leave to cool in the water – the custard will happily set there – then chill for 4 hours. To serve, spoon the poached quince along with some of the syrup into deep bowls and plop a spoonful of custard next door.

Peach Jelly

The perfect ending to a meal on a hot summer's day. A lightly poached peach, bursting with sun-ripened flavour and set in a quivering jelly, makes an exquisite dessert. Serve with lightly whipped cream, sweetened with a touch of icing sugar.

SERVES 6

300ml water
200g caster sugar
juice of ¹/₂ lemon
200ml Cava
6 ripe peaches
5 gelatine leaves

Put the water, sugar and lemon juice in a pan wide enough to hold the peaches in a single layer and slowly bring to the boil, stirring until the sugar dissolves. Simmer for 2 minutes, until the liquid becomes slightly syrupy. Pour in the Cava and gently bring to the boil over a medium heat before carefully dropping in the peaches. Reduce the heat and poach the peaches until tender. A very ripe peach will cook in around 5 minutes. Remove the pan from the heat, transfer the peaches to a dish, then pour over the liquid and leave until cool enough to handle. Peel off the skin from the peaches, carefully halve them, removing the stones, and place the halves in 6 clear glass tumblers, where they will fit quite snugly.

Put the gelatine leaves in a bowl, cover them with cold water and leave to soften for about 5 minutes. Meanwhile, pour the liquid from poaching the peaches back into the pan and reheat gently. Take the softened gelatine leaves from the bowl, squeeze out excess water, then drop them into the hot liquid. Stir until completely dissolved. Carefully pour the liquid over the peaches, pushing them down so they are submerged. Leave the jellies until they have cooled completely, then cover and chill; they should be set within 2 hours.

Peach Jelly Trifle

The best trifles need to be simple – I've never been one for an over-adorned trifle. There's no need to confuse the flavours and, with fewer ingredients, they have a cleaner, sharper taste.

One of the advantages of a trifle is that the jelly can be prepared the day before – so, apart from making the custard, it's then just a quick assembly job before doling out and tucking in.

SERVES 8

1 packet of Savoiardi biscuits, or a small Madeira cake, sliced
1 small glass of sweet wine or sherry
½ quantity of Peach Jelly (see page 208)
250ml double cream

For the custard:
6 organic egg yolks
130g caster sugar
2 tablespoons arrowroot or cornflour
250ml full-fat milk
250ml double cream

To make the custard, beat together the egg yolks, caster sugar and arrowroot or cornflour until smooth and pale. Warm the milk and cream in a heavy-based pan until the mixture is just beginning to bubble around the sides. Pour it on to the egg mixture, whisking all the time, then return the mixture to the pan. Cook over a low heat, stirring constantly with a wooden spoon, until the custard has thickened. Pour into a bowl and lay cling film on the surface of the custard to prevent a skin forming. Leave to cool completely.

Meanwhile, take a large glass bowl and place the sponge fingers or cake over the bottom in a single layer. Sprinkle over the wine; the sponge will absorb it and go just a little bit soggy. Spoon the peach halves and their surrounding jelly on to the sponge base, even out the surface with the back of a serving spoon, then pour over the cold custard. Cover and chill for at least 4 hours.

When you are ready to serve, whip the double cream into soft peaks and spread it over the top of the custard in a thick layer. Now you can sprinkle over hundreds and thousands, if you like. Childish, I know, but fun.

Baked Rice and Jam

Creamy and sweet, baked rice is the epitome of comfort food and always a hit on my pudding list. Choose a jam that is sharp and tart to offset the sweetness of the rice: raspberry or cherry would be my first choice. Or try a fruit compote – simply combine your chosen fruit with a small amount of water, add sugar to taste and simmer over a medium heat until the fruit bursts. Adding a vanilla pod or some orange or lemon zest to the rice will also enliven it.

Rice pudding needs a long, slow bake and some protection from the heat, so to that end I always bake it in a cast iron casserole dish.

SERVES 6–8

50g unsalted butter
100g Arborio rice or other short grain rice
500ml full-fat milk
500ml double cream
75g caster sugar
a pinch of sea salt
jam, to serve

Preheat the oven to 140°C/275°F/Gas Mark 1. Place a cast iron casserole dish over a medium heat and gently melt the butter in it. Add the rice, stirring well to coat all the grains in the butter, then add the milk, cream, sugar and salt and bring it all slowly to the boil. Stir the mixture well again, as the rice has a tendency to lump together at this point, then place the dish in the oven. Bake for 2 hours, or until the rice has absorbed the liquid and is soft, though still with a little bite. Remove from the oven and let it sit for 15 minutes, before serving in deep bowls with a dollop of your favourite jam.

Strawberry Shortcake

This recipe transforms a humble afternoon-tea favourite into an elegant, light dessert. It's adapted from Nigella Lawson's strawberry shortcake – a fantastically simple dish that really works. You could use any berries you can get your hands on: try raspberries, blackberries, or even gooseberries cooked with a touch of sugar. Their keen flavour works so well with the softness of the cream and the sweet bite of the shortbread.

SERVES 6

450g strawberries
2 tablespoons caster sugar
250ml double cream
icing sugar for dusting

For the shortcake
325g plain flour
$\frac{1}{2}$ teaspoon salt
1 tablespoon baking powder
65g caster sugar, plus 2 tablespoons for sprinkling
125g cold unsalted butter, diced
1 large organic egg
125ml double cream

First make the shortcake. Sift the flour, salt and baking powder into a wide bowl and mix in the sugar. Toss in the butter and, working quickly, rub it into the flour with your fingertips until the mixture resembles breadcrumbs. Mix together the egg and cream, then little by little, pour them into the bowl, working them in with a round-bladed knife or a metal spatula. When the mixture has come together, turn it out on to a lightly floured board and roll it into a disc about 2cm thick. Then, with the aid of a glass or coffee cup around 8cm in diameter, cut out as many discs as you can (you will need 6 for this pudding), pulling together any offcuts, which can be rolled again and then cut into shape.

Place the cakes on a baking tray lined with baking parchment, then put them into the fridge to rest for half an hour. Preheat the oven to 220°C/425°F/Gas Mark 7. Sprinkle the 2 tablespoons of sugar over the top of the shortcakes, place them on the middle shelf of the oven and bake for 10–15 minutes, until golden.

In the meantime, halve or quarter the strawberries, depending on their size, shake the sugar over them and leave to macerate.

To serve, lightly whip the cream until it forms soft peaks. Slice the cakes in half – I use a serrated bread knife for this, as the pressure of a regular blade could cause the cakes to crumble. Place each bottom half on a serving plate, top with a generous spoonful of strawberries and a dollop of cream, then pop on the lid. Finish with a dusting of icing sugar.

Raspberry Ripple Semifreddo

Italy's classic semifreddo is the best way I know of making ice cream without the gadgetry. Smart and simple, this frozen dessert has more in common with a parfait than an ice cream. Like a conventional ice cream, it has a light custard as its base, but it's the whipped cream and egg white that hold it firm, with no need for churning in an ice-cream maker.

The base is standard, so the flavours can be changed on a whim. You can substitute any fruit purée for the raspberries or even fold through crushed nuts or melted chocolate.

SERVES 4–6

4 organic eggs, separated
60g caster sugar, plus extra for sweetening the raspberries
150ml sweet wine (a sticky dessert wine is perfect)
250g raspberries
lemon juice to taste
300ml double cream
130g icing sugar

The first thing you need to do is make a sabayon, so put a pan of water on the stove, bring it to a simmer and choose a heatproof bowl that will fit comfortably over the top. Put the egg yolks, caster sugar and wine in the bowl and whisk with a balloon whisk or a handheld electric beater until they are smooth and pale yellow. Place the bowl over the pan, making sure it doesn't touch the water, and whip the mixture, just as if you were whipping cream, over the simmering water until the eggs are thick and foamy; the mixture should form thick ribbons when you lift the whisk from the bowl. Remove from the heat and leave to cool.

Purée the raspberries in a food processor and add a squeeze of lemon juice and enough caster sugar to sweeten them slightly – though leave them a little tart to offset the sweetness of the sabayon. Pass the purée through a fine sieve into a jug and set aside.

Whip the cream until it forms soft peaks, then fold in the cooled sabayon. In a separate bowl, whisk the egg whites until they form soft peaks. Add the icing sugar, beating until you have a soft, glossy meringue. Carefully fold the meringue into the cream mixture – you need to keep it as airy as possible – and then drizzle in a thin stream of raspberry purée, gently stirring it in until you have a ripple effect. Freeze for at least 6 hours, preferably overnight.

Sticky Toffee Pudding with Butterscotch Sauce

A retro favourite often found on the gastropub menu, sticky toffee pudding is heaven for the sweet-toothed diner. It's an extremely easy pudding to make, taking no more than 5 minutes and a short series of blasts in a food processor before baking. I always cook sticky toffee pudding in metal dariole moulds. The heat that the metal generates as it cooks gives the outside of the pudding a thin, chewy crust.

SERVES 4

150g dates, chopped
1 teaspoon bicarbonate of soda
250ml boiling water
50g unsalted butter, plus extra for the moulds
150g caster sugar
1 organic egg
200g self-raising flour
1 teaspoon baking powder

For the butterscotch sauce
200g soft brown sugar
200g unsalted butter
200ml double cream

Preheat the oven to 180°C/350°F/Gas Mark 4. Put the chopped dates into a bowl with the bicarbonate of soda and pour over the boiling water. This will soften the dates and make the pudding a little less chewy.

Beat together the butter and sugar, either in a food processor or by hand, until white and creamy. Mix in the egg, followed by the flour and baking powder. Beat the dates and their liquid into the batter.

Liberally butter 4 metal dariole moulds and pour in the mixture, filling them two thirds full so the sponge has room to rise. Place the puddings on a tray and bake on the middle shelf of the oven for 20–25 minutes, until they are deep brown and puffy.

Meanwhile, make the sauce. Gently heat all the ingredients in a pan until the sugar and butter have melted. Turn up the heat, bring to the boil, then cook until rich and dark.

Carefully unmould the hot puddings – you may need to run a knife around the inside of the moulds to do this – and divide them between bowls. Pour over the butterscotch sauce and serve with cream.

Black Forest Gâteau

Probably the ultimate Seventies cliché but before you smirk, just remember what's involved in this classic dessert: chocolate, cherries and cream, it's a dream combination. I'd love to see this fantastic pudding placed firmly back on pub blackboards. I could even start my own campaign, the Black Forest Gâteau one maybe...

SERVES 8

2 tablespoons kirsch or brandy
450ml double cream
1 tablespoon caster sugar
80g plain chocolate

For the cake
5 organic eggs
150g caster sugar
100g plain flour
50g cocoa powder
50g unsalted butter, melted and cooled

For the cherries
400g can of black cherries in syrup or 500g ripe red cherries
120g caster sugar
juice of 1 lemon

Preheat the oven to 180°C/350°F/Gas Mark 4. Butter and flour a 24cm springform cake tin, or line it with baking parchment.

For the cake, put the eggs and sugar into a mixing bowl and whisk until they are thick and creamy; they should form a thick ribbon when the whisk is lifted from the mixture. Sift the flour and cocoa powder into another bowl to combine them, then lightly sift them again on to the egg mixture. Fold them in thoroughly but lightly with a large metal spoon or a spatula and then drizzle in the melted butter, folding that through too. Pour the batter into the cake tin and bake for 15–20 minutes, until the cake feels springy to the touch. Leave to cool in the tin for 5 minutes before turning it out on to a wire rack to cool completely.

If you are using fresh cherries, then this is the time to prepare them. Wash them under the cold tap, then put them in a stainless steel saucepan with the sugar and lemon juice. Cover with a tight-fitting lid and simmer over a low heat for 10 minutes, until they are soft and have given off a lot of juice. Remove the cherries with a slotted spoon and leave on a plate to cool, then pop out the stones.

Slice the cake horizontally into 3 layers and sprinkle the lower 2 layers with the kirsch or brandy and a tablespoon or so of the cherry syrup. Whip the cream with the caster sugar until it forms soft peaks (you could add a touch more booze at this point, if you wish). Spread the 2 lower layers of the cake with half the cream and dot two thirds of the cherries over the top. Sandwich the 2 layers together, put on the top layer and then cover the top and sides with the rest of the cream. Grate the chocolate directly over the top of the cream and press a little over the sides. Decorate with the remaining cherries.

Steamed Golden Syrup Pudding

The perceived wisdom is that it takes hours to make a steamed pudding – trotting back and forth into the kitchen to top up the steamer and not even being able to see how it is progressing since it is covered with layers of fiddly paper. This can be true of larger steamed puddings, but at the Fox we avoid any fuss by making individual puddings and steaming them in a bain marie. This recipe is absolutely foolproof and takes only minutes to prepare. Best of all, the puddings rise like a sponge before your eyes and take only a fraction of the time to cook. It is essential to serve them with lashings of custard.

SERVES 4

50g unsalted butter, softened
100g caster sugar
a pinch of sea salt
60ml milk and 1 large organic egg
100g self-raising flour
8 tablespoons golden syrup

For the custard
5 organic egg yolks
2 tablespoons caster sugar
1 teaspoon plain flour
500ml full-fat milk

Preheat the oven to 180°C/350°F/Gas Mark 4. Prepare your bain marie by half filling a roasting tin with hot water and placing it on the middle shelf of the oven.

Throw all the ingredients apart from the golden syrup into a food processor and whiz until you have a smooth batter; this should take only about a minute. If the batter looks too thick to pour easily, just add a little more milk.

Lightly grease the dariole moulds with a little softened butter and pour 2 tablespoons of golden syrup into the bottom of each one. This may seem like a lot of syrup but the sponge will soak up most of it. Pour the batter into the moulds, place them in the bain marie and bake for 20 minutes; the puddings should have risen in the centre, split ever so slightly and be lightly browned.

Meanwhile, make the custard. Whisk the egg yolks, sugar and flour together in a bowl until smooth and pale. Warm the milk in a heavy-based saucepan until the surface just begins to ripple. It's important not to let the milk boil; apart from making a mess of the stove, it would change the flavour and consistency.

Pour the warmed milk on to the eggs and sugar, whisking as you go, then pour the mixture back into the pan. Place the pan over the lowest possible heat and stir constantly with a wooden spoon until the custard has thickened enough to coat the back of the spoon. Strain through a fine sieve into a glass bowl or jug.

To serve, unmould each pudding into a bowl and spoon over the custard.

Buttermilk Pudding

This recipe comes courtesy of Harry Lester from London's Anchor and Hope. I had the pleasure of working with Harry, first at the Eagle and then at the Fox, before he left to set up the Anchor and Hope with Jonathon Jones and Rob Shaw in 2003. This is what Harry has to say about his pudding:

'Many of us have eaten panna cotta but the puddings from the past, like junket and buttermilk pudding, have somehow become neglected. Buttermilk pudding is lighter than its counterparts and is more like an indulgent after-dinner yoghurt (in fact it always reminds me of Chambourcy Nouvelle). It is straightforward to make and appeals to everyone – children and adults alike. Although it is lovely eaten on its own, at the Anchor and Hope we always serve it with a fruit of the season: sliced oranges with a hint of caramel in winter; cherries with a splash of kirsch in summer.'

SERVES 6

1/2 vanilla pod
300ml double cream
110g caster sugar
a strip of lemon zest
4 gelatine leaves
600ml buttermilk

Slit the vanilla pod lengthways and scrape out the seeds with the tip of a knife. Place the pod and seeds in a pan with 100ml of the cream, plus the sugar and lemon zest. Gently warm the mixture over a low heat until the sugar has melted, being careful not to let it come to the boil. Remove from the heat. Soak the gelatine leaves in cold water for about 5 minutes. When they are completely soft, squeeze out the excess water and drop them into the warm cream mixture, stirring until they melt in. Leave to cool.

Remove the lemon zest and vanilla pod from the cooled cream and stir in the buttermilk. In a bowl, whip the remaining cream until it forms soft peaks. Gently fold in the buttermilk mixture.

Line 6 individual pudding moulds or ramekins with cling film and pour in the mixture. Cover and refrigerate; they should be set in around 3 hours. Turn out into bowls, remove the cling film and serve.

Lemon Tart

The classic lemon tart. Over the years this tart has wended its way from modest French bistros through to fine dining restaurants, finally finding a place on many gastropub menus. A refreshing end to any meal, it would be quite improper of me not to include a recipe here.

SERVES 6–8

8 organic eggs
300g caster sugar
200ml double cream
juice and grated zest of 4 lemons
icing sugar for dusting
crème fraîche, to serve

For the pastry
225g plain flour
50g caster sugar
115g fridge-cold unsalted butter, diced
2 organic eggs
40ml milk

To make the pastry, put the flour and sugar into a food processor and whiz until completely combined. Add the butter and pulse until it has just mixed in; you're looking for a fine breadcrumb texture. Add one of the eggs and, with the machine running, pour in the milk. Stop the machine as soon as the pastry forms a ball. Scrape out the dough, pat it into a disc, then wrap in cling film and chill for 1 hour.

Roll out the pastry on a lightly floured board and use to line a 24cm loose-bottomed tart tin. Return to the fridge and leave it to rest for another hour.

Preheat the oven to 180°C/350°F/Gas Mark 4. Prick the pastry base all over with a fork, cover it with greaseproof paper and weight it down with dried beans, or ceramic baking beans if you have them. Bake on the middle shelf of the oven for 15 minutes, then remove the paper and beans. Return the pastry case to the oven for 5 minutes, until the base is firm and golden. Beat the remaining egg, brush the pastry base with it, then return it to the oven for 3 minutes (this will ensure there are no cracks).

For the filling, whisk together the eggs and sugar until pale and thick, then lightly beat in the cream, lemon juice and zest. Don't beat too hard or the eggs are liable to thicken. Pour the mixture into a jug and leave it to settle for 1 minute, then skim off any bubbles from the surface. Reduce the oven temperature to 140°C/275°F/Gas Mark 1.

The easiest way to finish the tart is to place the tart tin on a baking tray and put the tray on the middle shelf of the oven. This way you don't have to carry a full liquid tart to the oven and risk spilling it.

Pour the filling into the pastry case, going slowly to ensure that none of it falls into the gap between the pastry and the tin. Carefully push the tray back into the oven and bake the tart for

30–35 minutes. It is done when the surface is soft and slightly springy and has a tiny wobble in the centre, around the size of a 10 pence piece. Leave to cool for at least 30 minutes before serving, or after it comes to room temperature, chill in the fridge. Serve with a dusting of icing sugar and a dollop of crème fraîche.

Crème Caramel

An elegant and enduringly popular dessert, crème caramel is simplicity itself to make. Taking up no more than half an hour of your time, its only drawback is that you have to wait until the next day for the caramel bottom to melt before you can devour it. It makes the ideal pudding for a dinner party or to follow a light lunch.

SERVES 6

½ vanilla pod
600ml full-fat milk
4 organic eggs
2 organic egg yolks
120g caster sugar

For the caramel
120g caster sugar
70ml water

To make the caramel, put the sugar and water in a small, heavy-based saucepan and place it over a low heat, swirling it around until the sugar has dissolved. Then turn up the heat and let it boil vigorously for about 5–7 minutes, until you have a dark caramel. Carefully pour the caramel into 6 dariole moulds or ramekins, 150ml in capacity, and place them in a baking tray.

Preheat the oven to 160°C/325°F/Gas Mark 3. Slit the vanilla pod open lengthways, scrape out the seeds and put both pod and seeds in a pan along with the milk. Gently bring the milk to a simmer, never letting it come to the boil, and whisk the vanilla seeds through the milk. Turn off the heat and leave to infuse for 5 minutes.

Beat the eggs, egg yolks and sugar together in a bowl until pale and thick, then pour in the hot milk, whisking all the time to combine. Strain the mixture through a fine sieve into a jug, skim off any bubbles that form on the surface, then pour the custard into the moulds containing the caramel. Boil a kettle full of water. Place the baking tray on the middle shelf of the oven and pour enough boiling water into the tray to come three quarters of the way up the sides of the moulds. Carefully push the tray back into the oven and bake for 30 minutes, until the custard has just set. It should be light and springy, with a tiny wobble in the centre.

Remove from the oven and leave the caramels to cool in the tray before chilling overnight in the fridge. To serve, run a butter knife around the side of each mould to loosen the crème caramel and invert it on to a small plate.

Rhubarb and Apple Crumble

Quintessential gastropub fodder, the humble crumble is a leading light on innumerable pub blackboards and the perfect pudding for a cool evening.

As a rule, I tend to use a tart eating apple as the base of my crumbles. I feel that Bramleys and other cooking apples need far too much sugar to make the pudding palatable. Another tip is to make the crumble mixture beforehand as, like pastry, it needs to rest to ensure that it doesn't shrink while cooking.

When rhubarb is out of season, feel free to substitute berries or any other fruit you fancy.

SERVES 6

6 large, tart apples, such as Granny Smith or Cox's
250g rhubarb
150g caster sugar

For the crumble
200g plain flour
100g fridge-cold unsalted butter
100g soft brown sugar

First up is the crumble mix. Don't be tempted to use a food processor for this; the fast action of the blades could render the mixture into balls of dough. Instead, sift the flour into a wide bowl and coarsely grate in the butter. This is made vastly easier if you continually dip the stick of butter into the flour, lightly coating it, so the butter doesn't stick to the grater or slip out of your hand. Rub the butter into the flour with your fingertips until the mixture resembles fine breadcrumbs, then stir the sugar through it. Cover the bowl and leave to rest in the fridge for 30 minutes.

Preheat the oven to 190°C/375°F/Gas Mark 5. Peel and core the apples and cut them into slices 1cm thick. Place in a large bowl. Trim the ends off the rhubarb, then cut it into slices 5mm thick and add to the bowl. Pour in the sugar and toss vigorously to coat.

Butter a 1-litre baking dish and put the fruit in it. Sprinkle over the crumble mixture, making sure it covers the fruit evenly and comes right up to the sides. Place the dish on the middle shelf of the oven and bake for 35–40 minutes, until the fruit is soft and bubbling and the top is golden brown. Leave to cool slightly for 5 minutes, then serve with cream, ice cream or custard.

Summer Pudding

For me, this is the star of all British puddings and the high point of the British summer. There is a great tradition of bread puddings in the UK – bread and butter (the first and probably the most popular), then ribsticking puddings filled with spices and dried fruit, plus apple charlottes and brown bread ice cream.

There are two essential points to note about summer pudding. First, it shouldn't be overly sweet, so the initial step is to achieve the requisite tartness. Currants, particularly blackcurrants, are mandatory – the burst of flavour as they hit the palate is crucial. Temper this with redcurrants and raspberries, and just enough sugar to take the edge off. A purist would use only these three fruits, though I like to throw a handful of blackberries into the mix too. I never use strawberries, they're far too sweet.

The second crucial thing is the bread you use for the casing. No white sliced here, please, it just seems to go slimy and doesn't fully absorb the juice from the fruit. Instead I would choose a good white sandwich loaf, which I'd slice myself to get the thickness just right – no more than a centimetre.

SERVES 6

250g redcurrants
150g blackcurrants
450g raspberries
50g blackberries
125g caster sugar
80ml water
6–7 slices of white bread

Pull the currants from their stalks. Put them in a heavy-based saucepan with the raspberries, blackberries, sugar and water. Place over a low heat, give it a good stir and bring to a simmer. Cook gently for 4–5 minutes, until the sugar has completely dissolved and the fruit has softened and released a good amount of juice. Remove from the heat and leave to cool.

Cut the crusts from the bread, then cut a circle out of one slice to fit the base of a 1-litre pudding basin. Slice the rest into fingers 2cm wide. Dip the circle of bread into the pan of fruit until it has soaked up a little of the juice, then place it in the basin. Now dip the bread slices into the juice and fit them around the sides of the bowl, overlapping them slightly so there are no gaps. Spoon the fruit into the bowl, pour over the remaining juice and place the rest of the bread fingers over the top. Cover the bowl tightly with cling film and place a saucer on top – one that fits snugly inside the rim – then weight that down with a can or two. Put the bowl in a dish to catch any leaky juices and chill for 12 hours or overnight.

To serve, run a knife around the edge of the basin to dislodge the pudding, place a platter over the top and quickly turn the bowl and platter over. Give it a little shake and the pudding will plop out on to the platter. Cut into wedges and serve with thick cream.

Blood Orange Posset with Tuiles

An old-fashioned English pudding that is a precursor to syllabubs and fruit fools, a posset is simply a set cream, and it couldn't be easier to make. Originally it was made as a drink in medieval times, using milk curdled with wine, beer or lemon. Through the years, however, cream, eggs and spices were added, even biscuits, which turned it into an early trifle.

I love to make possets with blood oranges. Their tartness offsets the cream beautifully and the vibrant reddish flesh lends an attractive pale orange hue. Serve with a crisp tuile biscuit. Tuiles are named after their resemblance to round roof tiles, or tuiles in French. They take their distinctive shape from being draped over a rolling pin while they are still warm, then left to cool and set.

SERVES 6

850ml double cream
250g caster sugar
juice of 3 blood oranges

For the tuiles
75g icing sugar
50g plain flour
2 organic egg whites
50g unsalted butter, melted

To make the tuiles, combine the icing sugar and flour in a food processor and, with the machine running, pour in the egg whites and melted butter. Whiz for no more than a minute, until you have a smooth paste. At this point you can refrigerate the mixture until you are ready to cook the biscuits.

Preheat the oven to 180°C/350°F/Gas Mark 4. Put a sheet of baking parchment on a baking tray. Place a teaspoon of the mixture on it and squash it down lightly with the back of the spoon. Continue with more of the biscuit mixture, making sure you leave enough room for the biscuits to spread – I usually leave about 8cm between them. Bake for 8–10 minutes, until the biscuits are golden brown around the edges but still pale in the middle. Leave them to rest for 1 minute on the tray, then carefully peel each one off with a spatula and drape it over a rolling pin or bottle to cool completely. This only takes about 5 minutes, giving you plenty of time to get on with another batch. The biscuits will keep for about 3 days in an airtight container.

To make the posset, place the cream, sugar and blood orange juice in a heavy-based saucepan, give them a good stir, then place the pan over a low heat until the sugar has dissolved. Raise the heat and bring to the boil. Now reduce the heat as low as possible and simmer for 2 minutes. Leave the cream to cool for 5 minutes, then pour it into wine or coupe glasses. When it is completely cold, put it in the fridge to set – this should take a couple of hours. Serve with the tuiles.

Lemon Delicious

Even though it is of British origin, this pudding is a much-loved Australian staple. Everyone there with even the slightest interest in cooking has a recipe. If you come across it in a gastropub here in the UK, the chances are there's an Antipodean in the kitchen. Unlike conventional steamed puddings it's what's known as a self-saucing pudding, miraculously separating during baking to form a light-as-a-feather sponge sitting on top of a pool of hot, tart lemon curd. Delicious.

SERVES 6

60g unsalted butter
220g caster sugar
grated zest of 1 lemon
3 organic eggs, separated
50g self-raising flour
280ml milk
juice of 2 lemons

Preheat the oven to 180°C/350°F/Gas Mark 4. Butter a 1-litre ovenproof dish.

Put the butter, sugar and lemon zest in a food processor and blend to a smooth, pale paste. Quickly whiz in the egg yolks, then add the flour and milk alternately until you have a batter. Scrape down the sides of the bowl and give the batter another quick whiz before blending in the lemon juice. Transfer the mixture to a clean bowl.

In a separate bowl, whisk the egg whites until they form stiff peaks. Gently fold a third of the egg white into the batter and when that is fully incorporated, fold in the remaining whites. Pour the mixture into the prepared dish and stand it in a deep roasting tin. Pour in enough hot water to come around half way up the side of the dish. Bake on the middle shelf of the oven for 45–50 minutes, until the top is golden and set like a sponge. Leave the pudding to rest for 5 minutes, then serve with thick cream.

Treacle Tart

I find this pudding almost tooth-numbingly sweet, but it's a huge favourite on the pub menu. Sometimes, just for a change and to give the tart a little bit of extra intensity, I substitute black treacle for the golden syrup – it is treacle tart after all.

SERVES 6–8

140ml golden syrup
juice and grated zest of 1 lemon
130g fresh white breadcrumbs
1 teaspoon ground ginger

For the pastry
225g plain flour
50g caster sugar
115g fridge-cold unsalted butter, diced
2 organic eggs
40ml cold milk

To make the pastry, put the flour and sugar into a food processor and whiz until completely combined. Add the butter and pulse until it has just mixed in; you're looking for a fine breadcrumb texture. Add one of the eggs and, with the machine running, pour in the milk. Stop the machine as soon as the pastry forms a ball. Scrape out the dough, pat it into a disc, then wrap in cling film and chill for 1 hour.

Roll out the pastry on a lightly floured board and use it to line a 24cm loose-bottomed tart tin. Return it to the fridge and leave to rest for another hour.

Preheat the oven to 180°/350°F/Gas Mark 4. Prick the pastry base all over with a fork, cover it with greaseproof paper and weigh it down with dried beans, or ceramic baking beans if you have them. Bake on the middle shelf of the oven for 15 minutes, then remove the paper and beans. Return the pastry case to the oven for 5 minutes, until the base is firm and golden. Beat the remaining egg and brush it over the pastry base, then return it to the oven for 3 minutes (this will ensure there are no cracks).

Warm the golden syrup in a pan over a low heat until it has completely melted. Stir in the lemon juice and zest, breadcrumbs and ginger. Pour the mixture into the pastry case and bake for 25–30 minutes, until the filling has set and is a darkish golden brown. Serve warm or cold, with thick cream.

Roast pumpkin

wild mushroo

Clams, white

Smoked hadd

Cod & tartar

Bits and Pieces

Mayonnaise
Tartare Sauce
Marie Rose Sauce
Green Mayonnaise
Aioli
Anchoïade
Harissa
Seville Orange Marmalade

Mayonnaise

Probably the most versatile sauce that you can have in your repertoire, mayonnaise is so simple to make that you could almost do it with your eyes closed. It is an essential accompaniment to many of the dishes in this book, particularly seafood, and I find it's just handy to have a pot in the fridge to serve with raw vegetables or cold meat and salad. Mayonnaise also provides a base for numerous other sauces, such as tartare, Marie Rose or a simple fresh herb mayo.

You can easily make mayonnaise by hand but a food processor makes the job quick and even easier.

3 organic egg yolks
1 tablespoon Dijon mustard
1 tablespoon lemon juice
350ml sunflower or vegetable oil
sea salt and freshly ground black pepper

Blend the egg yolks, mustard and lemon juice together in a food processor until well combined. With the machine running, gradually add the oil in a thin, steady stream until you have incorporated it all. If the mayonnaise is too thick, add a little warm water to thin it down. Season with sea salt and black pepper and adjust the acidity with a little more lemon juice to taste.

Tartare Sauce

Make the mayonnaise as above, then stir in 1 tablespoon chopped capers, 1 tablespoon chopped gherkins, 1 small shallot, finely chopped, 1 tablespoon chopped parsley, 1 teaspoon chopped tarragon or dill and 1 grated hard-boiled egg.

Marie Rose Sauce

Make the mayonnaise as above, then stir in 2 tablespoons of tomato ketchup, 1 teaspoon of Worcestershire sauce, a few drops of Tabasco and a squeeze of lemon juice.

Green Mayonnaise

Make the mayonnaise as above, then fold through 2 tablespoons of chopped parsley, chives and tarragon and season with an extra touch of lemon juice.

Aioli

A seemingly indispensable sauce in all gastropubs, aioli goes with pretty much everything. I don't muck about when I make aioli and, in proper Provençal style, I use enough garlic to give a good head rush and stinky breath for a few hours. If this isn't to your taste, feel free to reduce the garlic content. The only way my version differs from the French one is that I cut the olive oil with half vegetable oil so the sauce isn't too bitter.

3 organic egg yolks
1 tablespoon Dijon mustard
6 garlic cloves, chopped
juice of ½ lemon
200ml vegetable oil
200ml olive oil
sea salt and freshly ground black pepper

Blend together the egg yolks, mustard, garlic and lemon juice in a food processor. Start adding the oils gradually in a slow steady stream, just like mayonnaise, until they have been completely incorporated. Season with sea salt and black pepper, then add a little more lemon juice if you like a sharper flavour.

Anchoïade

The quantities below make quite a large batch but, stored in an airtight container in the fridge, it will keep for up to 2 weeks. You can use it to dress spring greens, broccoli and bitter leaves such as trevise and dandelion, or simply spread it on toast for a tasty snack.

150g anchovies in oil, drained
2 garlic cloves, chopped
2 teaspoons Dijon mustard
1 tablespoon sherry vinegar
1 teaspoon thyme leaves
350ml extra virgin olive oil
freshly ground black pepper

Put the anchovies, garlic, mustard, vinegar and thyme in a food processor and blend to a smooth paste. With the machine running, slowly add the olive oil in a thin, steady stream, as if you were making mayonnaise. Season with a grind of black pepper.

Harissa

A heady, aromatic paste found throughout the Middle East, harissa is a fantastic partner for grilled meat or fish. It is also particularly good folded through braised vegetables or spooned into leek and potato soup. Diluted with a little more olive oil, it makes an excellent marinade for chicken and squid before it hits the barbecue.

You can make the harissa as hot as you like but be careful not to overdo it, as the heat of the chilli can cancel out the freshness of the herbs.

1 teaspoon cumin seeds
a small bunch of mint
a small bunch of coriander
2 garlic cloves, peeled
6 red chillies, seeded
½ teaspoon sea salt
1 teaspoon dried mint
150ml extra virgin olive oil

Warm a small frying pan, then add the cumin seeds and dry roast them over a low flame until they start to release their aroma. Tip the warm seeds on to a plate and leave to cool. Pick the leaves from the fresh mint, roughly chop the coriander, stalks and all, and place them in a food processor along with the rest of the ingredients. Whiz everything together until you have a smooth paste. The harissa will keep in an airtight container in the fridge for up to 2 weeks.

Seville Orange Marmalade

Around the second week of January, the first boxes of Seville oranges start arriving from Spain. As they have such a short season – only about a month – I try to make the most of the time they are available. A strip of peel will find its way into a rich beef stew, while the juice is combined with eggs and sugar to make an orange curd to fill tarts. With the whole fruit, I make batches of marmalade – wonderful alongside a chunk of Cheddar or Lancashire cheese. A teaspoon of this tangy marmalade in the bottom of a steamed syrup pudding adds a refreshing zing.

2kg Seville oranges
4kg preserving sugar or caster sugar

Wash the oranges, put them in a large stainless steel saucepan and cover with water. Bring to the boil, then cover and simmer for about 1½ hours, until the skins are soft and can be easily pierced with a sharp knife. Remove the oranges from the liquid, keeping the liquid to one side, and leave them on a plate to cool. When they are cool enough to handle, cut them in half and scoop the pulp, including the pips, into a colander. Press down hard with the back of a spoon to push the pulpy mixture through the holes, then add this to the cooking liquid. This pulp is full of pectin and will help to set the marmalade.

Now slice the orange skins, thick or thin, depending on how chunky you like your marmalade, and add them to the pot. Stir in the sugar and place the pan back on the heat. Stir until the sugar has dissolved, then boil over a high heat for 15–20 minutes, skimming off any whiteish scum that rises to the surface.

To test whether the marmalade is at setting point, drop a teaspoon of it on to a fridge-cold saucer and leave it for about a minute – if it sets, it's ready, otherwise continue boiling and test it again after a few minutes.

Leave the hot marmalade to cool in the pan for 30 minutes, stirring every few minutes – this ensures that the strips of peel are evenly distributed through the jelly and won't just fall to the bottom. Ladle into sterilised jars (see Green Tomato Chutney on page 194 for how to sterilise jars), cover and store in a cool, dry place for at least 1 month before opening.

Index

A

B

C

D

E

F

Acknowledgements

For making this book happen, there are so many people who have helped me along the way that I hardly know where to start, so I'll start with the people most important to me:

My parents, Kevin and Joan, and David Tatham, who watched over, encouraged and put up with me through all the distractions the writing brings; my sisters and brother also, for just being there.

Jon, Matt and Meg at Absolute Press for giving me another opportunity to write, and Jane Middleton for such patience and great editing. Tom Norrington-Davies and Jason Lowe help me enormously and for that I truly thank them. And Mike Belben, what can I say, thank you for all the support through the years, it's been great.

Many thanks to the following:
Jorge Cardoso, Sam Waterhouse, Ed Nassau-Lake, Tovi and all of the chefs who have passed through the Fox kitchen; Joe Kelly and the entire bar staff, past and present.

Thank you to the chefs and landlords who took time out of their considerable workload to contribute to this book: Jonathon Jones and Harry Lester from the Anchor and Hope, Jonny Haughton and Pete Richnell from the Havelock Tavern, Martin Kroon and Kevin Cooper from the Cat and Mutton, Charlie and Amanda Digney from the King William, and Scott Wade from the Gun.

Lastly, thank you:
Claire Leigh-Browne and Rob McClymont, Barney Desmazery, Pat and Peter Tatham, Ben Woodcraft, Barry Hadden, Wendy Sayell, all at Neal's Yard Dairy, Robin Hancock and Ben Wright from Wright Bros, Paul and Terry Bailey from Lennards and Fred and all at McKanna Meats.

About the author

Trish Hilferty has worked both in the UK and in her native Australia, learning her craft in some of the best restaurants in the world. Her stint as chef at London's legendary gastropub, The Eagle, set her on the road to gastropub superstardom. As head chef of The Fox Dining Room in Shoreditch, she scooped the prestigious 'Tio Pepe London Gastropub of the Year' award in 2005. Her first cookery book, *Lobster & Chips*, was published in 2005 to great critical acclaim, receiving the Gourmand World Cookbook Award for 'Best English UK Single Subject Food Book'.